LAW AND THE NATIONAL LABOR POLICY

Industrial Relations Monographs of the
Institute of Industrial Relations

No. 1. *Due Process on the Railroads: Revised Edition,*
by Joseph Lazar.

No. 2. *Right-to-Work Laws: A Study in Conflict,*
by Paul Sultan.

No. 3. *The Knights of Labor in Belgium,*
by Léon Watillon. Translated and with an introduction by Frederic Meyers.

No. 4. *Inside a Sensitivity Training Group,*
by Irving R. Weschler and Jerome Reisel.

No. 5. *Law and the National Labor Policy,*
by Archibald Cox.

LAW AND THE NATIONAL LABOR POLICY

By Archibald Cox

GREENWOOD PRESS, PUBLISHERS
WESTPORT, CONNECTICUT

Library of Congress Cataloging in Publication Data

Cox, Archibald, 1912-
Law and the national labor policy.

Reprint. Originally published: Los Angeles : Institute of Industrial Relations, University of California, 1960. (Monograph series / Institute of Industrial Relations, University of California, Los Angeles ; no. 5)
Includes bibliographical references.
1. Labor laws and legislation--United States.
I. Title. II. Series: Monograph series (University of California, Los Angeles. Institute of Industrial Relations) ; no. 5.
KF3369.3.C66 1983 344.73'01 82-20930
ISBN 0-313-23794-8 (lib. bdg) 347.3041

Reprinted in 1983 by Greenwood Press
A division of Congressional Information Service, Inc.
88 Post Road West, Westport, Connecticut 06881

Printed in the United States of America

10 9 8 7 6 5 4 3 2 1

Foreword

The Institute of Industrial Relations is pleased to offer, as the fifth in its Monograph Series, *Law and the National Labor Policy,* by Archibald Cox. In substance this volume constitutes a series of five lectures on this topic that Professor Cox delivered at the University of California, Los Angeles, under the sponsorship of the Institute of Industrial Relations in November–December, 1959.

Archibald Cox is Royall Professor of Law at the Harvard Law School. He is a distinguished authority on labor law who has written widely on that subject. Professor Cox is the author of the Massachusetts anti-injunction and arbitration statutes. He served as Chairman of the Advisory Panel on Labor-Management Relations Law to the Senate Committee on Labor and Public Welfare. He was the principal adviser to Senator John F. Kennedy of Massachusetts in drafting the Kennedy bill, one of the main antecedents of the Labor-Management Reporting and Disclosure Act of 1959. Professor Cox discusses that statute at length in *Law and the National Labor Policy.*

The Institute is grateful to the Division of Research of the Graduate School of Business Administration at UCLA for a grant to underwrite the publication of this monograph. Mrs. Anne P. Cook edited the manuscript. The cover was designed by Marvin Rubin.

The viewpoint expressed is that of the author and is not necessarily that of the Institute of Industrial Relations or of the University of California.

BENJAMIN AARON, *Acting Director*
Institute of Industrial Relations
University of California, Los Angeles

Preface

These lectures were delivered at the University of California, Los Angeles, in November and December, 1959, under the auspices of the Institute of Industrial Relations. The text has been slightly revised in order to correct inadvertent errors. The second lecture was too long for complete delivery. However, I have not attempted to change the style from what seemed appropriate to oral delivery, nor have I delayed preparation of the manuscript in order to take account of developments between the delivery of the lectures and February, 1960, when they went to press.

Since the lectures attempted to present a rounded summary of critical problems in the development of the national labor policy, they deal with subjects which I have discussed in more detail in scattered publications. I felt free, therefore, to draw upon my earlier writing where it was pertinent to the subject at hand. The fourth lecture draws heavily upon my article "Reflections Upon Labor Arbitration," 72 Harv. L. Rev. 1482 (1959). Since the second lecture was prepared contemporaneously with a paper delivered before the Labor Law Section of the Minnesota State Bar Association, some parts of it also appear in 44 Minn. L. Rev. 257 (1959).

I am indebted to the Institute, especially to Acting Director Benjamin Aaron and Associate Director Irving Bernstein for making available both the time and facilities required for the preparation of these lectures and to the staff of the Institute for their assistance in preparing the manuscript for the press.

Archibald Cox

Langdell Hall
February, 1960

Contents

Chapter 1

The Evolution of Labor-Management Relations Law

To understand our labor laws one must comprehend the genius of our labor unions. The basic urge which leads men to organize, the spark which gives labor unions life and the power of growth under favorable conditions, is the human drive toward self-advancement. During the past century the industrial revolution and the disappearance of the frontier transformed the United States from a nation of farmers, artisans, and shopkeepers into a community of wage earners, many of them laboring in mines, mills, and factories. The same forces brought together vast corporate aggregations of property. The individual worker lost the power to bargain effectively with his employer. Job security became a major worry because employment provides the wage earner's only source of livelihood and avenue of self-advancement. Gathering thousands of employees into integrated factories concentrated vast power in the hands of the managers and their subordinates—a power all too easily exercised in arbitrary fashion. The rule of law to which the western world aspires in political life became an ideal of the industrial community. Men also began to lose the pride of accomplishment which characterized the ancient artisanship. Reduced to routine tasks and often counted as mere units of labor, they craved a share in industrial decisions affecting them.

Every industrial society faces these problems. Some countries adopt extensive social legislation. Others turn to the nationalization of industry or even violent revolutions. In the United States the traditions of a frontier community bred distrust of government and confidence in self-determination. The fluidity of society prevented the growth of a class-conscious proletariat. The success of the American dream deterred radical reformers. The dominant philosophy discouraged political action. When the Knights of Labor collapsed in 1886, trade-union leaders turned from humanitarianism and reform to efforts to improve the position of the wage earner through his job, here and now. Self-help—

organizing the unorganized and bargaining collectively—became the union worker's creed. The strike, the boycott, and the picket line became his primary weapons.

Thus oriented, the American labor movement made two principal demands upon the law. One was for the right to form, join, and assist labor organizations and, through them, to bargain collectively with employers. The second was for the maximum freedom to use economic weapons—strikes, boycotts, picketing, and other concerted activities—to spread unionization and wring concessions from employers. Unionization and collective bargaining would have little value without the right to use these economic weapons, for although negotiation has its own compulsions, few "voluntary" agreements are executed in the absence of economic power. Concerted activities were also important methods of organizing new unions in the face of employer opposition. Without the right to strike, the genius of the American labor movement would be changed and, in consequence, we should have to revise our system of industrial relations.

By the last quarter of the nineteenth century the law recognized the privilege of organizing labor unions without civil or criminal liability,[1] but the second demand brought the unions into conflict with the courts. Courts of equity have traditionally issued injunctions against a conspiracy to injure a man's trade or business and therefore, if an employer could convince the court that a strike or boycott was a conspiracy, the court would order it stopped. Strikes, picketing, boycotts, indeed all the economic weapons of organized labor, involve concerted action intended to injure the employer's business until he yields to the union's demands. According to the common law, "concert of action is a conspiracy if its object is unlawful or if the means used are unlawful."[2] The definition sounds plausible but the term "unlawful" was used in a Pickwickian sense to denote not something contrary to law but any objective which the courts disapproved. For example, an employer could lawfully sign a closed-shop contract; if he did, the courts would enforce it; but in many states it was an unlawful object of a strike.[3]

Justice Holmes offered a better analysis: "[W]hen a plaintiff proves that several persons have combined and conspired to injure his business, and have done acts producing that effect, he shows temporal damage and a cause of action, unless the defendants prove some ground of

[1] Commonwealth v. Hunt, 4 Metc. (Mass.) 111 (1842).

[2] Truax v. Corrigan, 257 U.S. 312, 327 (1921).

[3] See, *e.g.*, Fashioncraft, Inc. v. Halpern, 313 Mass. 385, 388, 48 N.E.2d 1, 3–4 (1943).

excuse or justification."[4] The formula emphasizes that the "true grounds of decision are considerations of policy and of social advantage,"[5] but it provides no more definite answers than the conspiracy doctrine. If justification were lacking—or, in the language of conspiracy, if the objective were unlawful—the strike, boycott, or picketing was enjoined in order to protect the employer's business.

Most courts took a narrow view of the permissible objectives of concerted action, which can be described best by narrating the facts of a single case. By 1910 the United Mine Workers had organized the coal mines in Ohio and Pennsylvania, but West Virginia was a nonunion field. Direct labor costs were a large factor in the price of coal, and the market was highly competitive. If the union scale were raised, the increased price of Ohio and Pennsylvania coal would allow the low-wage, nonunion mines in West Virginia to capture a larger share of the market, thereby forcing a cut in the union scale or causing unemployment. The UMW countered by sending organizers into West Virginia. When they secured enough members at the Hitchman mine, a strike was called to unionize the company. Hitchman had exacted from each miner a promise not to join a labor union while he worked for the company. When the organizer persuaded a Hitchman miner to join, he was advised to avoid discharge by concealing his membership. The Supreme Court held that the organizer's activities were an unjustified interference with the contracts and that support of the strike should be enjoined because the UMW had no interest in wages, hours, or working conditions at the Hitchman mine.[6]

So long as the *Hitchman* case stood, it would be impossible to organize nonunion mines in the face of an employer's opposition. So long as there were important nonunion mines, it would be exceedingly difficult to improve wages and conditions of employment. The same situation prevailed in other industries, and other courts reached like conclusions.[7] The labor injunction was an insuperable obstacle to union organization in the face of active employer opposition. The main thrust of the labor movement in relation to the law, indeed of the entire effort to solve workers' problems in an industrial society, was therefore aimed at establishing freedom to use the strike, the boycott,

[4] Vegelahn v. Guntner, 167 Mass. 92, 105, 44 N.E. 1077, 1080 (1896).

[5] 167 Mass. at 105, 44 N.E. at 1080.

[6] Hitchman Coal & Coke Co. v. Mitchell, 245 U.S. 229 (1918).

[7] *E.g.*, Alco-Zander Co. v. Amalgamated Clothing Workers, 35 F.2d 203 (E.D. Pa. 1929); Simon v. Schwachman, 301 Mass. 573, 18 N.E.2d 1 (1938). *Contra*, Exchange Bakery & Restaurant, Inc. v. Rifkin, 245 N.Y. 260, 157 N.E. 130 (1927).

the picket line, and other economic weapons. Every restriction which it is proposed to put upon strikes today would curtail a freedom which the labor movement strove to achieve as its staff of life for two generations.

Because there is so much current discussion of applying the Sherman antitrust law to labor unions, it is worth pausing to note that the Sherman Act was the basis of many labor injunctions. The Act provides: "Every contract, combination in the form of trust or otherwise, or *conspiracy* in restraint of trade or commerce among the several States . . . is hereby declared to be illegal."[8] Since the word "conspiracy" was held to incorporate the common-law definition, the statute gave employers a right to enjoin through the federal courts any strike, boycott, or picketing which the courts disapproved, provided that it interfered with interstate commerce. Whatever may be the present potentialities of the Sherman Act, history shows that it was applied to labor unions in the past not to preserve competition in the sale of goods or to prevent the creation of monopolistic power, but as a vehicle for the judicial formulation of a policy toward strikes, boycotts, and picketing.[9]

I

The right to use concerted activities unimpeded by federal law was won in 1932 when Congress enacted the Norris-LaGuardia Act, the first of the four statutory cornerstones of the current national labor policy.[10] Section 4 immunized union organization, concerted refusals to work or patronize, inducement to strike or boycott, and picketing from restraint by injunction regardless of the objectives and later, as the result of judicial decisions, from attack by criminal prosecution or civil action for damages.[11] The courts retained the power to enjoin violence or wrongs to tangible property, but Section 7 corrected many faults in the old equity procedure and Sections 7 and 8 together had the effect of postponing resort to the courts until all other methods of settling the dispute and preserving the peace had been exhausted. The Act is broad enough to cover every controversy in the federal courts involving the conflicting interests of management and labor.[12]

[8] 26 STAT. 209, 15 U.S.C. § 1. Emphasis supplied.

[9] A more elaborate discussion will be found in Cox, *Labor and the Anti-Trust Laws*, 104 U. PA. L. REV. 252 (1955).

[10] 47 STAT. 70, 29 U.S.C. §§ 101 *et seq.* Although the Norris-LaGuardia Act has not been modified or repealed, its impact has been altered by the Taft-Hartley amendments to the National Labor Relations Act. See pp. 15–18 *infra.*

[11] United States v. Hutcheson, 312 U.S. 219 (1940).

[12] Section 13 defines a labor dispute to include "any controversy concerning terms

The Norris-LaGuardia Act had practical economic origins. It was enacted at the bottom of the Great Depression. Employees were weak, ill-paid, and working under deplorable conditions. Its sponsors believed that the workers' bargaining power could be enhanced and their earnings and working conditions improved by concerted action. Labor injunctions were obstacles; therefore they deprived the courts of power to issue injunctions.

Perhaps these economic forces were alone sufficient to carry the day, but the Norris-LaGuardia Act also rested upon closely reasoned theory. The central proposition was that law served no useful purpose in labor disputes, save possibly to protect tangible property and preserve public order. Its philosophical underpinning was the belief that the government should not resolve labor disputes or substitute its wage or price determinations for private contracts in a free market. Union organization, strikes, boycotts, and picketing were held to be part of the competitive struggle for life, which society tolerates because the freedom is worth more than it costs. Justice Holmes stated the thesis forty years earlier in the dissenting opinion in *Vegelahn v. Guntner:*

> I have seen the suggestion made that the conflict between employers and employed was not competition, but I venture to assume that none of my brothers would rely upon that suggestion. If the policy upon which our law is founded is too narrowly expressed in the term "free competition," we may substitute free struggle for life. Certainly, the policy is not limited to struggles between persons of the same class competing for the same end. It applies to all conflicts of temporal interests.[13]

The single garage which a small community can support may be ruined by a competitor. A price war between major oil companies may drive marginal distributors into bankruptcy. The nonunion employees willing to work at the Hitchman mine for wages below the union scale could cause loss to the UMW members without liability. The same principle should govern, it was said, when the UMW members engaged in economic action which advanced their interests. If the operator's business suffered from the strike, the loss should be *damnum absque injuria.* If the nonunion employees lost employment or were forced to join a union not of their own choosing, that too was the price of a free community in which each may pursue his own economic advantage.

---

and conditions of employment, or concerning the association or representation of persons in negotiating, fixing, maintaining, changing or seeking to arrange terms or conditions of employment, regardless of whether or not the disputants stand in the proximate relation of employer and employee."

[13] Vegelahn v. Guntner, 167 Mass. 92, 107, 44 N.E. 1077, 1081 (1896).

The law should not intervene on either side of the contest. Furthermore, the protagonists of this theory held that since the circle of competing interests is not confined to a single employer and his own employees as a matter of fact, it should not be confined in legal theory.[14]

In recent years the law has increasingly regulated the weapons with which men pursue the free struggle for life. The Sherman Act, for example, limits mergers and other business combinations because of the costs of the concentration of excessive economic power. The use of labor's economic weapons could never be completely justified in the name of competition without reference to the environment, but in 1932 the workers were underdogs and the community had little to fear from the power of association and concerted activity. Furthermore, the weapons which the community permits one group to use must be determined with reference to the methods of self-help available to its competitors. In the United States the opposition of employers to labor unions has been far more bitter than in Great Britain or the Scandinavian countries, which have comparable labor movements. Threats of reprisal, discriminatory discharges, blacklists, labor spies, and professional strikebreakers were common weapons. So long as employers made war upon unions, the strike, the boycott, and the picket line were the unionist's only countermeasure.

The argument that law should play no role in industrial relations gained strength from other criticisms of the labor injunction. Anyone could see that the lawfulness of the activities of the United Mine Workers in the *Hitchman* case depended upon an appraisal of the values and costs of spreading union organization. If unions might lawfully strike for a closed shop in California but not in Massachusetts,[15] if organizational picketing was forbidden in Ohio but permitted in New York,[16] were the judges applying rules of law or issuing personal fiats? Ought not the law upon such basic social and economic issues be made by the people through elected representatives?

The objection to judicial policy-making was sharpened by the accusa-

[14] Of course a trained economist would distinguish concerted action to secure union recognition or higher wages from the concept of competition between numerous traders in a free market which stimulates technological innovation and holds down the price, although it is far from clear that the judges ever confined the justification for business conduct to competition in this narrow sense. Mogul Steamship Co. v. McGregor, Gow & Co., 23 Q.B. Div. (1889).

[15] *Compare* J. F. Parkinson Co. v. Building Trades Council, 154 Cal. 581, 98 Pac. 1027 (1908), *with* Plant v. Woods, 176 Mass. 492, 57 N.E. 1011 (1900).

[16] *Compare* Crosby v. Rath, 136 Ohio 532, 25 N.E.2d 934 (1939), *with* Exchange Bakery & Restaurant, Inc. v. Rifkin, 245 N.Y. 260, 157 N.E. 130 (1927).

tion that the courts had one law for business combinations but another for labor unions. When a combination of employment agencies agreed to drive their competitors out of business by refusing to furnish seamen to any vessel whose owner did not deal exclusively with members of the combination, the court upheld the combination in the name of fair competition;[17] but when a labor union—a combination of employees—refused to furnish men to a contractor unless he agreed to hire all his employees through the union, the same court issued an injunction.[18] Decisions like the *Hitchman* case seemed to display either prejudice or a lack of elementary economics.

The most serious fault was that injunctions were essentially repressive in the sense that they required the employees to desist from using the only effective forms of self-help, yet did nothing to solve the underlying problems that drove men to strike. The *Hitchman* injunction thwarted the United Mine Workers but did not improve the lot of the coal miners. The famous *Debs* injunction may have checked the nationwide spread of economic paralysis as a result of the great railroad strike of 1894, but the Pullman workers were left to suffer in the squeeze between successive wage cuts and the constant rents and prices in the company villages; nor did courts stop to observe that the immediate occasion of the strike was a discriminatory layoff of union committeemen.[19] In forbidding secondary boycotts the law did not ask about the wages or working conditions which the union was seeking to alleviate nor inquire into their effect upon competitors. I do not mean to imply that the judicial process is suited to these inquiries. The point is simply that the grant or denial of an injunction bore little relation to the merits of the underlying dispute. Coupled with distrust of other forms of government regulation, this seemed to prove that the law could make no contribution to industrial relations.

The thesis of the Norris-LaGuardia Act is the philosophy underlying organized labor's claim to the rights to strike, to boycott, and to picket. They are the rocks upon which the American labor movement is founded. In asserting them union workers posit a free competitive society. There is no other labor movement in the world with the same degree of attachment to the social and economic system which surrounds it. Workers claim the rights to strike, boycott, and picket as a

[17] Bowen v. Matheson, 14 Allen (Mass.) 499 (1867).

[18] Plant v. Woods, 176 Mass. 492, 57 N.E. 1011 (1900).

[19] Contrast the opinions in United States v. Debs, 64 Fed. 724 (C.C.N.D. Ill. 1894), and *In re* Debs, 158 U.S. 564 (1895), with the Report of the U.S. Strike Commission on the Chicago Strike, 1894.

defense against aggression from competing interests and as the best means of self-advancement. Today society must sometimes qualify these rights in the public interest. Each qualification makes inroads upon the philosophy of freedom and self-determination. There is a critical point beyond which society cannot curtail the rights without having to construct a substitute system of industrial relations which will supply in some other form—probably through government—the protection and opportunities which American workers have thus far found in freedom of association and concerted activities.

It is also worth noting that the labor injunction was no less government interference than legislative, executive, or administrative regulation, for the judiciary is an arm of the government. The Norris-LaGuardia Act introduced the only period of unqualified laissez faire in labor relations.

For a time it seemed possible that the philosophy of the Norris-LaGuardia Act would find its way into constitutional law. During the next decade the Supreme Court held a series of state court injunctions unconstitutional under the Fourteenth Amendment upon the ground that picketing "must now be regarded as within that liberty of communication which is guaranteed to every person by the Fourteenth Amendment against abridgement by a State."[20] A few lower courts, noting that the picket line, like a strike or boycott, is an economic weapon, concluded that all these peaceful activities "are fundamental human liberties which the State may not condition or abridge in the absence of grave and immediate danger to the community."[21] Within a few years, however, the Supreme Court, having marched up the hill, marched down again under the pressure of the developments which next claim attention.[22]

II

Although the prevailing sentiment in the labor movement prior to the 1930's sought only to remove the governmental obstacles to union organization and collective bargaining, there was always a minority which sought affirmative legal protection against employers. The concept flourished during World War I[23] and was kept alive in railway labor

[20] Carlson v. California, 310 U.S. 106, 113 (1940). See also Thornhill v. Alabama, 310 U.S. 88 (1940); American Federation of Labor v. Swing, 312 U.S. 321 (1941).

[21] Stapleton v. Mitchell, 60 F. Supp. 51, 61 (D. Kan. 1945), *appeal dismissed*, 326 U.S. 690 (1945).

[22] Cox, *Strikes, Picketing and the Constitution*, 4 VAND. L. REV. 574 (1951). The last important decision upon the constitutional status of picketing is International Brotherhood of Teamsters v. Vogt, Inc., 354 U.S. 284 (1957).

[23] NATIONAL WAR LABOR BOARD, PRINCIPLES AND RULES OF PROCEDURE 4 (1919); U.S. BUREAU OF LABOR STATISTICS, BULL. NO. 287, NATIONAL WAR LABOR BOARD 264 (1921).

laws during the 1920's.[24] It fitted naturally into the grand scheme of the National Industrial Recovery Act of 1933, for the NRA sought to organize all industry through trade associations, labor unions, and codes of fair competition that would eliminate cutthroat competition and other wasteful practices and so stabilize, if not raise, the price level; while on the employee side wages were raised, hours were shortened, and industrial homework, child labor, and other sweatshop practices were eliminated. Even after the NRA collapsed, the Roosevelt Administration's interest in encouraging unionization and collective bargaining continued. In 1935 the enactment of the Wagner Act[25] supplied a permanent legal foundation for the right of employees to organize and bargain collectively through representatives of their own choosing.

The heart of the Wagner Act was Section 7, which guaranteed employees three rights: (1) freedom to form, join, and assist labor organizations, (2) freedom to bargain collectively with the employer through representatives of their own choosing, and (3) the right to engage in concerted activities.

The right to organize was central. Section 8 prohibited specific anti-union practices such as discriminatory discharges and the establishment of company-dominated unions; it also contained a general prohibition against interference with the rights guaranteed by Section 7. Section 8(5), which imposed upon employers an affirmative duty to bargain collectively with the representatives of their employees, was included because the denial of recognition was a method of discouraging unionization.[26] In creating this duty, however, Congress carried the political principle of majority rule into labor-management relations—a unique North American development which has had unforeseen but far-reaching consequences in the evolution of public policy, although in 1935 it seemed to require only the development of administrative machinery for conducting elections in the appropriate bargaining unit. The task was delegated to a National Labor Relations Board,[27] which was also charged with preventing and correcting employer unfair labor practices.[28]

---

[24] These statutes culminated in the Railway Labor Act of 1926 which gave the rights to organize and bargain collectively full legal status. 44 STAT. 577.

[25] National Labor Relations Act, 49 STAT. 449 (1935), hereafter cited as NLRA.

[26] The legislative background is discussed from this point of view in Cox and Dunlop, *Regulation of Collective Bargaining by the National Labor Relations Board*, 63 HARV. L. REV. 389 (1950).

[27] NLRA § 9.

[28] NLRA § 10.

We need not concern ourselves yet with the large body of law created in the administration of the Wagner Act, but it seems useful to state the basic principles of the national labor policy at this stage in its development.

1. The American system of industrial relations should be based upon strong unions and free collective bargaining. The function of government is to encourage collective bargaining. The role of law is to protect the exercise of the rights to organize and to bargain collectively against interference by employers.

2. The law should not intervene in labor disputes by restricting strikes, boycotts, or picketing in aid of unionization or collective bargaining. These rights are indispensable to industrial workers in a free competitive society. If the rights were denied, the system of industrial relations would have to be changed.

There was an inherent contradiction in these two principles which would eventually require the qualification of the second. The Norris-LaGuardia and Wagner Acts were consistent in that both were aimed at encouraging the growth of unions. They operated in different spheres in that the one removed impediments to self-help on the part of employees, while the other placed restrictions upon employers. Nevertheless, giving employees legally protected rights of self-organization and collective bargaining made fundamental changes in the premises which theretofore supported the unrestricted use of concerted activities as organizing weapons.

The view that the law had no useful role to play in labor disputes unless there was violence or destruction of property became untenable after legal restrictions were imposed upon the conduct of employers in relation to union organization. No civilized jurisprudence could tolerate the inconsistency of requiring a company to bargain exclusively with a union certified by law while doing nothing to stop a rival union from injuring the same employer in order to secure exclusive recognition for itself.

The ideas of freedom of choice and majority rule are antithetical to the Holmesian philosophy of competition. So long as self-interest and the value of freedom of action were thought to justify harm, it made little difference whether the unorganized employees joined a union because they wished, because the employer forced them in order to save his business, or because the power of the union to deprive them of jobs by shutting down the business left no viable alternative. Any sacrifice of their desire or of the employer's interests was a cost of the free struggle for life. "Top-down organizing" was a simple and direct method of driving low-cost nonunion goods from the market and eliminating the competition of nonunion labor. Many unions adopted, and still sincerely believe in, this technique but it is plainly inconsistent with the NLRA ideal of employee self-organization without interference by employers. Economic pressure upon the employees may also be inconsistent with the ideal of freedom of choice, although this is a closer question.[20]

A union's need for economic weapons with which to extend its organization was reduced by the inhibitions which the Wagner Act imposed upon employers, and the force of an employer's claim that the law should protect his business was correspondingly increased.

More than twenty years have been required to resolve these ideological inconsistencies between two of our basic labor laws. The inconsistency was hardly significant until economic changes and the abuses of a few enormously powerful labor barons shattered the public image of the downtrodden worker. The resolution, while not complete, is found largely in the partial restraints imposed upon organizational picketing in the Labor-Management Reporting and Disclosure Act of 1959. These restraints will be explained and appraised in the next chapter.

3. The Wagner Act left substantive terms and conditions of employment entirely to private negotiation. The Act neither established wages, hours, or other conditions of employment nor authorized an administrative tribunal to determine them. It provided no governmental machinery for the adjustment of disputes concerning substantive terms and conditions of employment. The basic theory of the law in its original form, as today, was that the arrangement of substantive terms and conditions of employment is a private responsibility.

4. The sponsors of the Wagner Act held that the creation and enforcement of the rights to organize and bargain collectively were the best method of achieving industrial peace without undue sacrifice of personal and economic freedom. The conclusion was based upon a carefully articulated argument. The prohibition of employer unfair labor practices and the legal compulsion to bargain with any union designated by a majority of the employees in an appropriate unit would reduce the number of strikes for union recognition. Previously, when an employer refused to bargain, the union's only recourse was to strike; under the Act it could secure legal redress. Collective bargaining would also tend to reduce the number of strikes over substantive issues by causing employers and employees to dig behind their prejudices and

[20] This question is discussed in the second lecture.

exchange their views to the point where they reached agreement or at least discovered that the area of rational disagreement was so narrow that it was cheaper to compromise than to battle. Recognition, experience in bargaining, and the resulting maturity would bring a sense of responsibility to labor unions. As early as 1902 a federal commission had found:

> Experience shows that the more full the recognition given to a trades union, the more businesslike and responsible it becomes. Through dealing with businessmen in business matters its more intelligent, conservative, responsible members come to the front and gain general control and direction of its affairs. If the energy of the employer is directed to discouragement and repression of the union, he need not be surprised if the more radically inclined members are the ones most frequently heard.[30]

Collective bargaining, it was also said, would eliminate low wages and adverse working conditions. Wages, hours, and other terms and conditions of employment would be fixed by mutual consent rather than the employer's dictate. The resulting agreements would establish a rule of law, being the measure of both the employer's and employees' rights and obligations. The correction of these basic causes of strikes should reduce their occurrence.

But no one supposed that strikes would be eliminated. Often the force which makes management and labor agree is an awareness of the costs of disagreement. Freedom to strike, the threat of a strike, and possibly a number of actual strikes are indispensable parts of a national labor policy based upon the establishment of wages, hours, and other terms and conditions of employment through private collective bargaining. Whether the country can always afford this policy was not then in question.

5. Perhaps it is also significant that the Wagner Act was designed to raise the national wage level and that in the 1930's price increases were not unwelcome. There was no occasion to ask whether constant wage increases with the attendant risks of a cost-push inflation are an inescapable cost of collective bargaining as a system of industrial relations.

III

Between 1935 and 1947 labor unions grew and collective bargaining spread rapidly with the aid and encouragement of the federal government. In 1935 fewer than 4 million workers belonged to labor unions. In 1947 there were over 14 million union members—roughly four times

[30] Anthracite Coal Strike Commission Report, S. Doc. No. 6, 58th Cong., Spec. Sess. 31, 61 (1902).

as many. Two thirds of the workers in manufacturing were covered by union agreements and about one third in nonmanufacturing industries outside of agriculture and the professions. In some industries, such as coal mining, construction, railroading, and trucking, over four fifths of the employees worked under collective bargaining agreements.

Although government policies do not alone explain this phenomenal development, they exerted important influence. The legal protection available under the Wagner Act curbed antiunion tactics. For the government to prosecute an employer for unfair labor practices gave psychological impetus to unionization.

When World War II approached, it was plain that the United States could not become the arsenal of democracy without the wholehearted cooperation of organized labor, and the surest method of obtaining cooperation was to give unions a large role in directing the mobilization and allocation of our national resources. The role of unions in government and the high praise which government officials bestowed upon the labor movement encouraged unionization. Labor's participation reached a peak in the organization of the tripartite War Labor Board, on which the public, industry, and organized labor were equally represented. Once a union became the bargaining representative, War Labor Board policies encouraged the development of procedures confirming and strengthening its role in the plant—use of company bulletin boards, preferential seniority for shop stewards, grievance machinery with participation by the union, and arbitration of unsettled grievances. The union organizer could plausibly sign up new members with the argument, "It's your patriotic duty; the government wants you to join a union."

By 1947 the public was worried about the power of unions. Its worry was partly an irrational but widespread fear of "the labor bosses." John L. Lewis and the United Mine Workers had carried on two long strikes in defiance of the government during wartime, ending only when the government granted substantial concessions. In 1946 a great wave of strikes shut down the steel mills, automobile assembly plants, packing houses, the electrical products industry, the east and west coast seaports, and a few public utilities. Today it seems plain that this phenomenon simply marked release from wartime restrictions. In 1947 there were many who saw the danger of nationwide stoppages as a threat to the social system.

But if some of the fear was irrational, there were also careful observers sympathetic to organized labor who perceived the need for measures halting the abuse of power. Their bill of particulars might have included six specifications:

1. Too many strikes were called under circumstances threatening serious injury to public health or safety—strikes in the coal mines and in public utilities, for example.

2. Although corruption had not been uncovered as high in the union movement as during the subsequent McClellan investigation, it was plain that some so-called "labor unions" were little more than rackets.

3. Strikes and picketing were too often marked by violence organized and promoted by union leaders when peaceful measures failed to achieve their objective.

4. During the war many building trades unions refused to admit new members and charged exorbitant fees for issuing working permits to the employees attracted to the industry by defense construction. Later large projects were tied up for days while labor unions disputed each other's right to job assignments.

5. The secondary boycott had become an exceedingly powerful weapon. The International Brotherhood of Teamsters could tie up any business dependent upon trucking for supplies and outgoing shipments. The United Brotherhood of Carpenters through its control of construction projects could force a boycott of materials produced by any firm on which it desired to impose economic pressure. Secondary boycotts were also used as a method of controlling competition among employers in the product markets.

6. Abuses of power under closed- or union-shop contracts, although exceptional, gave force to the attack upon all union security agreements. A good many observers who saw merit in closed- and union-shop agreements felt the need for additional safeguards.

In 1947, as today, many business concerns continued to make war on labor unions despite the National Labor Relations Act. Others accepted the forms of collective bargaining under legal and economic compulsion, hoping that the tide would turn and they might some day be free from "the union." The irreconcilables were strengthened by the changing frontiers of union organization. People who genuinely sympathized with the plight of unorganized workers in mines, mills, and factories doubted the need for unions in wholesale and retail trades or office buildings where the business itself might be smaller and economically weaker than the union. In the South organized labor encountered a social and political system quite unlike industrial metropolises.

The Taft-Hartley Act,[81] the third of our four basic labor statutes, was enacted in 1947 as the product of these diverse forces—the offspring, one might say, of an unhappy union between the opponents of all collective bargaining and the critics of abuse of union power. The permanent contributions which the Taft-Hartley Act made to the national labor policy fall under several headings. Their most striking quality is the emerging challenge to the philosophy of self-help and freedom of competition.

1. The Taft-Hartley Act carried forward the fundamental rights to organize and bargain collectively, but the policy of encouraging the spread of union organization and collective bargaining yielded to official indifference. The change in emphasis was based on the belief that labor unions had become so strong that legislative action was required to redress the balance. This change and the further adjustments made in the summer of 1959 are considered in the second chapter but it is worth noting here that labor organizations with crushing economic power feel the consequences less than unorganized employees and weak unions struggling for survival.

2. The Taft-Hartley Act qualified the principle that labor should be free to use any peaceful economic weapons in support of union organization and the employees' demands in collective bargaining. Section 8(b) outlaws (i) secondary boycotts, that is, the refusal to work for employer A unless he ceases to do business with employer B, with whom the union has its real dispute, (ii) strikes to compel an employer to commit the unfair labor practice of discharging an employee for belonging (or not belonging) to a particular union, or of bargaining with the striking union after the NLRB has certified a different representative, and (iii) jurisdictional strikes over work assignments. But although its premise was qualified, the Norris-LaGuardia Act was neither amended nor repealed and many important conclusions embodied in its provisions remain part of the national policy. The statutory injunctions issued under the Taft-Hartley amendments differ from the old equity injunctions in four significant respects.

a. The basic questions of policy have been resolved by Congress instead of the judiciary.

b. There can be no private suits for an injunction. Control of the proceedings is vested in the National Labor Relations Board, a government agency. There is disinterested investigation before suit is brought, and the restraint is presented in its true light as an expression of public

[81] Labor Management Relations Act, 1947, 61 STAT. 136, hereafter cited as LMRA.

condemnation of the defendants' conduct rather than as a weapon in a private quarrel.

c. The points at which the Taft-Hartley Act revived legal intervention into everyday disputes are trivial in comparison to those it leaves untouched.

d. The law intruded only in areas where the overwhelming consensus of opinion condemns the unlawful conduct. This is clearly true of violence and strikes to compel the commission of unfair labor practices. While the jurisdictional dispute provisions are faulty, there is almost unanimous agreement upon the wisdom of outlawing jurisdictional strikes. Even in the field of secondary boycotts, there is quite general agreement that some of them should be forbidden by law; the debate is over where to draw the line.

3. The Taft-Hartley amendments bear evidence of doubt concerning the wisdom of placing unqualified reliance upon free private negotiation of terms and conditions of employment. When the Wagner Act was adopted, the collective bargaining process was assumed to be self-operating, perhaps with the aid of government mediation. The NLRB gradually extrapolated from the duty to bargain a body of decisional law requiring employers to negotiate upon specified subjects[32] and regulating, at least to some extent, the manner in which negotiations should be conducted.[33] The Taft-Hartley amendments impliedly ratified the trend of decisions. The amendments also gave further evidence of governmental concern for the manner in which negotiations are conducted, for they imposed a duty to bargain collectively upon labor unions and prescribed the procedure to be followed upon the reopening or expiration of a collective agreement.[34]

There was also worry over whether collective bargaining, even if regulated by law and aided by mediation, could always be relied upon to bring about the settlement of labor disputes in critical industries before they endangered the national health or safety. Unfortunately, the Act's sponsors were so thoroughly committed to avoiding government influence upon the terms of the settlement that they provided only a remedy reminiscent of the repressive injunctions of earlier years. The Act authorizes an eighty-day injunction against such a strike but offers no method of resolving the underlying controversy.[35] The problem is ripe for re-examination, and will be considered in the third chapter.

[32] Cox and Dunlop, *supra* note 26; Cox, *Labor Decisions of the Supreme Court at the October Term, 1957*, 44 VA. L. REV. 1057, 1074–1086 (1958).

[33] Cox, *The Duty to Bargain in Good Faith*, 71 HARV. L. REV. 1401 (1958).

[34] NLRA §§ 8(b)(3) and 8(d).

[35] LMRA § 209.

4. The administration of labor agreements was scarcely touched by law during the years in which management and labor were evolving the institutions necessary for mature collective bargaining. Collective agreements were negotiated without much regard to whether they were enforceable contracts or merely treaties resting upon mutual interdependence backed by moral force and fear of economic reprisals. Since disputes over the interpretation of agreements were bound to arise and there was need for a peaceful method of resolution, labor and management, with help from impartial experts, created an imaginative system of grievance arbitration, administered by private initiative and resting upon voluntary compliance without legal sanctions. History will mark the Taft-Hartley Act as the turning point at which law began to play a large role in contract administration. Section 301 provides that suits for violation of collective bargaining agreements in industries affecting commerce may be brought by or against a labor organization as an entity in an appropriate federal court. Its enactment made collective bargaining agreements enforceable contracts and encouraged both unions and employers to seek legal sanctions in situations in which they might otherwise have relied upon private arbitration, persuasion, or economic power. Unless Congress intervenes, the federal courts must now create a body of substantive and procedural law determining rights and duties under collective bargaining agreements without injuring the voluntary system of grievance arbitration.[36] This delicate problem is the chief topic of the fourth chapter.

5. Organized labor received one unexpected bonanza from the Taft-Hartley amendments. The federal system gives both Congress and the states power to regulate industrial relations. Until 1935 the power was exercised only by the states, except under the Sherman Act or in the case of interstate railroads. State law was concerned chiefly with the restriction of strikes, boycotts, and picketing. Many states declined to follow the philosophy of the Norris-LaGuardia Act, and since the Wagner Act did not deal with these subjects, state courts remained open to suits for injunctions. When the federal government entered these fields in 1947, it became necessary for the Supreme Court to decide whether the state and federal restrictions upon concerted activities should apply concurrently or the federal law should exclude state law from the same area. The Court ruled, wisely in my opinion, that the federal jurisdiction was exclusive because unrestricted application of state law would interfere with the effectuation of the national labor policy. The rule

[36] Textile Workers Union v. Lincoln Mills of Alabama, 353 U.S. 448 (1957).

protects labor activities wherever the Taft-Hartley restrictions upon strikes, boycotts, and picketing are less severe than those which would be imposed through state court injunctions, a condition which prevails in most states.[37] The nationalization of industrial relations was the single most important consequence of the Taft-Hartley amendments.

IV

The Labor-Management Reporting and Disclosure Act of 1959[38] marks the final legislative step in the evolution of the national labor policy. The most controversial sections deal with a familiar problem—how far should labor unions be permitted to resort to concerted economic activities in aid of unionization—but the primary significance of the new statute lies in the government regulation of the internal affairs of labor unions, an area not theretofore touched by legislation. When the federal government gave labor unions both legal and practical power as statutory bargaining representatives, it assumed an obligation to prevent abuse of the power. The regulations imposed in the summer of 1959 were another inescapable consequence of the Wagner Act.

For several years there had been growing concern about the relationship between the union and its members. The McClellan Committee hearings produced evidence of misconduct by the officials of a few unions ranging from embezzlement to illicit secret profits. There are signs that many members look upon their unions simply as service organizations to which they pay dues in return for higher wages, pensions, insurance, holidays, supplemental unemployment benefits, and other monetary advantages. Too few members attend meetings, and a fair proportion, I fear, are indifferent to the conduct of their officials so long as they continue to get higher wages and larger benefits.

Possibly this is enough, but I wonder whether labor unions which act simply as paid service organizations seeking higher dollar benefits are either fulfilling the needs of workers or can count upon the support of the community. Is business unionism's "more and more and more" a sufficient aspiration for the labor movement? Do individual men and women gain much by substituting a dictatorship of union officials for the erstwhile power of the boss? If one of the aims of collective bargaining is to give employees a chance to recapture freedom and individual

[37] Among the many discussions of the development of federal preemption are Cox, *Federalism in the Law of Labor Relations*, 67 HARV. L. REV. 1297 (1954), and Meltzer, *The Supreme Court, Congress and State Jurisdiction of Labor Relations*, 59 COLUM. L. REV. 6, 269 (1959).

[38] Pub. L. No. 86-257, 86th Cong., 1st Sess. (Sept. 14, 1959), 73 STAT. 519.

dignity by participating in decisions affecting their industrial lives, just as we participate through our political representatives in the decisions of government, then must not steps be taken to insure democracy within the labor movement and to protect individuals and minorities against the oppression not only of officials but even of a numerical majority of the members? In a nutshell, can any but a democratic union advance the ideals of individual responsibility, equality of opportunity, and self-determination? Or are the ideals to be abandoned?

Neither the law nor public policy can answer all these questions. The answers will ultimately come from within organized labor. The contributions which the national labor policy can make, including those offered by the Labor-Management Reporting and Disclosure Act, will be the subject of the final chapter.

Chapter 2

Public Policy Toward Union Organization

Public policy toward union organization is embodied not only in statutes, executive orders, and administrative and judicial decisions but also in countless informal expressions of governmental attitude. During the Roosevelt Administration union leaders were frequently invited to the White House for consultation; their pictures were taken with the President and they issued statements from the White House porch. This has not happened since President Eisenhower took office. The McClellan Committee hearings mar the reputation of the labor movement. A vigorous congressional investigation of the techniques used, and monies expended, in lobbying for right-to-work laws or to prevent unionization of the textile industry would arouse enthusiasm for union organization. Such manifestations of the prevailing governmental attitude toward labor unions have as much influence upon the prestige, and therefore upon the growth, of the labor movement as the formal exercise of governmental power.

The legal manifestations of public policy toward union organization, with which this chapter is primarily concerned, have two aspects: (1) regulation of the use of strikes, picketing, and other economic weapons as methods of organizing nonunion establishments, and (2) protection of organizational activities against interference from employers. Before discussing these subjects, however, it is essential to recall five salient facts concerning the present condition of the labor movement.

1. The struggle for union organization has not been completed. Despite the power of some unions there remain masses of unorganized workers who would benefit by collective bargaining. In the United States about half the employees engaged in manufacturing belong to labor organizations;[1] in Sweden, Denmark, and Norway, more than 90 per cent.[2] In the United States roughly 15.8 million workers out of the 64.8 million employed belong to unions affiliated with the American Federation of Labor and Congress of Industrial Organizations—about

[1] STATISTICAL ABSTRACT OF THE UNITED STATES 283 (1959).
[2] COMPARATIVE LABOR MOVEMENTS 119–120 (Galenson, ed. 1952).

25 per cent.[3] In Great Britain 42 per cent of the employed persons are union members.[4]

2. Collective bargaining is no longer spreading. In 1933, 11.5 per cent of the employees in nonagricultural establishments belonged to a labor union; in 1940, 27.2 per cent; in 1945, 35.8 per cent; but in 1956, only 33.7 per cent. In the twelve-year period 1935–1947 union membership increased fivefold; for the past twelve years there has been no increase.[5]

3. The distribution of union strength is very uneven. The latest figures available show that, in 1953, 27.2 per cent of the employees in New England's nonagricultural establishments and 39 per cent on the Pacific Coast belonged to unions, but only 18.3 per cent were members in the South Atlantic states despite the inclusion of the highly organized state of West Virginia. In North Carolina only 8.3 per cent were members, compared with 30.1 per cent in Massachusetts and 35.7 per cent in California.[6]

4. The wide variations in the extent of union organization between different industries are exemplified by the contrast between the automobile and textile industries. There are also great differences in the power of individual unions. No one expects the United Steelworkers suddenly to lose its bargaining power, but many locals of the Amalgamated Clothing Workers are struggling for existence.

5. Although part of American industry has accepted collective bargaining as a system of industrial relations, there remains an organized and determined opposition. Recently, in Henderson, North Carolina, a textile manufacturer forced a bitter, unsuccessful strike over a question so fundamental to collective bargaining as whether the grievance arbitration clause should be stripped from the Textile Workers' contract.

Even this hasty sketch should make plain the damage done by formulating policy upon an image of "the labor monopoly" resulting from the steel strike or of "the labor bosses" created by newspaper publicity concerning James Hoffa or John L. Lewis. Legislation enacted with the United Mine Workers or International Brotherhood of Teamsters in mind will continue to have unions like the International Ladies' Garment Workers or the Textile Workers as its victim unless Congress and also the executive, administrative, and judicial branches of the government take more account of the fact that there is not one labor problem

[3] The estimate in the text is taken from statistics prepared for the AFL-CIO Director of Organization. It is several years old but appears still to be roughly correct.

[4] Ministry of Labour Gazette, Vol. 62, No. 11 (November 1954).

[5] STATISTICAL ABSTRACT OF THE UNITED STATES 283 (1959).

[6] *Id.* at 237.

in the United States but many different problems in diverse areas and different stages of labor relations.

The nature of the legal process demands a degree of uniformity despite the variegated pattern of industrial relations. Federal statutes must apply uniformly to all geographical areas even though the measures most appropriate for sections where unions are strong are unsuited to communities in which unions are struggling for existence against organized and bitter opposition. There are also limits to permissible classification. Different as they may be, Congress cannot enact one law for the International Brotherhood of Teamsters, a second for the United Automobile Workers, and a third for the Textile Workers Union. The subtle, intangible factors which would enter into a perfectly wise, particularized judgment are often different from the relatively crude phenomena with which the law can deal with a modicum of efficiency. As an example, recall the gap between the criteria which governed the early issuance of labor injunctions and the underlying problems which workers were seeking to solve by strikes and boycotts.[7]

Thus, the policy-maker faces a dilemma; he cannot achieve the diversity of treatment required to meet the needs of management and labor in different industries without denying the demands of the legal system. There may be no perfect solution but in my opinion there is room for improvement. Congress has ignored cognizable differentiations in the drafting and administration of labor legislation. There has been too little willingness to make use of the adaptability and flexibility of the administrative process. These faults are least apparent in the legislative restrictions upon organizational picketing, which are the logical outcome of the enactment of the Wagner Act and can be made fair and workable with courageous administration. The dilemma is acute in the treatment of secondary boycotts, but we have neglected distinctions which the law could have managed and with more imagination we might perfect others. The most serious consequences, however, are the want of government encouragement for union organization and the weakening of legal safeguards against antiunion tactics by employers. The fear of excessive power, which explains, if it does not justify, some of the restraints imposed upon strong labor organizations in areas where collective bargaining is well established, should not have been allowed to influence the aspects of public policy primarily concerned with protection for the organizational activities of weak or incipient unions. The need for this protection is increased by restrictions upon such methods of self-help as organizational picketing and secondary boycotts.

[7] See pp. 2–7 *supra*.

I

The long controversy over organizational picketing resulted primarily from the basic inconsistency between the Norris-LaGuardia[8] and Wagner Acts.[9] Although both were enacted in the early 1930's to encourage the growth of unions, they could not stand together within a consistent legal system without major modifications. No civilized jurisprudence could lay duties upon an employer such as the obligation to bargain with a certified union and then deny him adequate legal protection when another union resorted to a strike, boycott, or picketing in order to compel their violation. The Wagnerian ideals of freedom of choice and majority rule are antithetical to the "dog-eat-dog" philosophy which justified the use of economic weapons by organized employees to secure their own self-interest regardless of the cost to others. The proscription of employer unfair labor practices diminishes the necessity for using economic weapons as methods of organization. While unions were weak, the paradox escaped attention, but it made changes in the law inevitable as soon as their growing power increased the effectiveness of economic weapons. Strikes, boycotts, and picket lines are most useful to organizations whose existing strength enables them to use the weapons effectively in extending their own membership or aiding other unions. The weapons have less use in the hands of weak unions and are valueless to unorganized employees until they achieve a measure of organization.

The impact of the Wagner Act was first manifested in Section 8(b)(4)(C), which was added by the Taft-Hartley Act.[10] The section provides that it shall be an unfair labor practice for a labor organization to induce employees to strike or refuse to perform their normal services with an object of requiring any employer to recognize or bargain with a particular labor organization if another representative has been certified. This prohibition is necessary to give effect to the principle of majority rule during the period for which a certification bars a new election; it protects the employer against economic pressure intended to compel him to violate the law or to punish him for compliance. The cases holding that minority strikes and picketing are prevented by a prior certification for an indefinite period[11] carry the rule beyond its

[8] 47 STAT. 70 (1932), 29 U.S.C. §§ 101 *et seq.*

[9] 49 STAT. 449 (1935), hereinafter cited as NLRA.

[10] 61 STAT. 136 (1947).

[11] Tungsten Mining Corp., 106 N.L.R.B. 903 (1953); Tungsten Mining Corp. v. District 50, United Mine Workers, 242 F.2d 84 (4th Cir. 1957); Parks v. Atlanta Printing Pressmen, 243 F.2d 284 (5th Cir. 1957).

justification. Once the employer is relieved of the legal duty to bargain with the certified union, the question is no longer whether the will of the majority should be protected; it becomes, what techniques are, or should be, open to a union which is now lawfully seeking to become the majority representative.[12]

In one respect Section 8(b)(4)(C) was obviously incomplete. A collective bargaining agreement with a representative freely designated by a majority of the employees in an appropriate bargaining unit bars an election for a reasonable period, usually two years.[13] Minority picketing for union recognition or organizational purposes during this period, like picketing during the first year of a certification, seeks to override the will of the majority and compel the employer to violate legal obligations. The Landrum-Griffin amendments filled the gap by adding Section 8(b)(7) to the NLRA, making it an unfair labor practice to picket for such purposes "where the employer has lawfully recognized in accordance with this Act any other labor organization and a question concerning representation may not appropriately be raised under section 9(c) of this Act."[14]

A certification carries a high degree of assurance that the incumbent union was the free majority choice. There is no such guaranty in a collective agreement. If the NLRB is content to be guided by formal appearances, Section 8(b)(7)(A) may become a refuge for unscrupulous employers and racketeer unions. The words of the amendment, read with appreciation of its rationale, invite a more penetrating inquiry. They prohibit the picketing only if the employer recognized the union "lawfully" and "in accordance with this Act." It is unlawful and contrary to the Act for an employer to grant exclusive recognition to a union which has not been designated by a majority of the employees in an appropriate unit or which is the beneficiary of an unfair labor practice.[15] A contract does not prevent raising a question of representation unless the union had an uncoerced majority at the time the contract was signed and there was no conflicting claim to recognition.[16] Section 8(b)(7)(A) can be made an effective instrument for carrying out the basic policies of the Act without damaging the legitimate interests of any bona fide union if these questions are carefully investigated by the

[12] This question is discussed at pp. 28–31 *infra*.

[13] 22 NLRB Ann. Rep. 18–19 (1957).

[14] Pub. L. No. 86–257, 86th Cong., 1st Sess. (Sept. 14, 1959), § 704(c).

[15] Bernhard-Altmann Texas Corp., 122 N.L.R.B. No. 142 (1959).

[16] There appears to be no exact precedent for this statement but most lawyers would acknowledge it to be indisputably true. See, generally, 22 NLRB Ann. Rep. 24 (1957).

General Counsel and thoroughly litigated in the district court and the NLRB before an injunction or a cease-and-desist order is issued.[17]

An understanding of the theory of the statute may correct two other technical faults. Section 8(b)(7)(A), read literally, would prohibit a union from picketing an employer in an effort to organize a unit of production workers if the employer had a contract with another union covering a unit of maintenance workers. It also speaks too loosely of inability to raise a question of representation under Section 9(c), which might literally cover any case in which the union could not prove that 30 per cent of the members desired it to represent them. Both faults can be corrected by focusing upon the basic rationale, which was that economic pressure aimed at compelling an employer to violate his duties to another labor organization should be made unlawful. This makes it clear that only the contract bar is material and that the prohibition does not go beyond picketing to organize, or secure recognition in, a bargaining unit in which an election is barred by the outstanding agreement.[18]

There are state court and NLRB decisions applying the foregoing rationale to picketing for recognition by a union which does not already represent a majority of the employees in the bargaining unit,[19] even though there is no existing contract or certification. Passing questions of state and federal jurisdiction, the verbal logic is impeccable. It is an unfair labor practice for an employer to sign a contract recognizing a union as the exclusive bargaining representative unless it has been designated by a majority of the employees in an appropriate unit;[20] therefore, if the union pickets after demanding a contract, the law forbids the employer to grant the pickets' demand. The logic breaks down if the union makes no demand for immediate recognition and pickets for the announced purpose of inducing the employees to join

[17] There is no necessary inconsistency between the above interpretation and the implications of the amendment to NLRA § 10(l) which directs the regional attorney not to apply for a temporary restraining order if a charge has been filed against the employer under § 8(a)(2). The proviso is applicable to all subdivisions of § 8(b)(7) and represents a compromise between the view that there should never be a temporary injunction where the employer was charged with any unfair labor practice and the argument that this would put it in the power of unions to stall injunction proceedings indefinitely. The above interpretation deals only with § 8(b)(7) and would seem to rest solidly upon its words.

[18] The impropriety of invoking the 30 per cent rule is further demonstrated by the fact that the Conference Report deleted from the House amendment a provision which would have prohibited picketing by a union which did not represent 30 per cent of the employees. See S. 1555, § 705(c), as passed by the House of Representatives.

[19] *E.g.*, Kenmike Theatre v. Moving Picture Operators, 139 Conn. 95, 90 A.2d 881 (1952).

[20] Bernhard-Altmann Texas Corp., 122 N.L.R.B. No. 142 (1959).

the union and the employer to sign a contract after a majority have become members, for this employer is not being asked to violate the statute. Consequently some courts permit "organizational picketing" while prohibiting picketing for recognition.[21]

The distinction seems foolish. Legal logic receives due obeisance, and a premium is put upon retaining clever counsel. Neither accomplishment can offset the loss of respect for law which follows such verbal distinctions. The employer, the union business agent and the employees would join in echoing Mr. Bumble's assertion that "the law is an ass, an idiot," but unhappily they could not follow the early English judge who corrected such an absurdity, saying that "it could not be the law, for I have so great veneration for the law as to suppose that nothing can be law which is not founded in honesty and common sense."[22]

The Landrum-Griffin amendments treat organizational and recognition picketing alike.[23] Apart from the provision mentioned above, the new rules rest upon two distinctions.

Picketing in any form is treated as a legitimate organizing weapon until the employees have expressed their wish in an NLRB election. Picketing is prohibited thereafter, except by a certified union, for the twelve-month period for which the law prohibits another election. To forbid picketing after a majority votes "No Union" expands the notion of freedom of choice beyond the Wagner Act's guaranty of freedom to choose a collective bargaining representative into freedom to have none; and it partially guarantees the freedom against economic pressure from unions as well as interference by employers. This expansion of the concepts of the Wagner Act is necessary to prevent a union in a key industry from using overwhelming economic power to attach other appropriate bargaining units as satellites. The Teamsters Union, for example, appears to have compelled employees to designate it as their bargaining representative against their wishes by threatening to use organizational picketing to destroy the business upon which their jobs depended.[24] The national labor policy should encourage collective bargaining but not at the cost of permitting powerful groups to destroy the right of self-determination.

[21] *E.g.*, Wood v. O'Grady, 307 N.Y. 532, 122 N.E.2d 386 (1954); Anchorage, Inc. v. Waiters and Waitresses Union, Local 301, 383 Pa. 547, 119 A.2d 199 (1954).

[22] Ashurst, J., in Pasley v. Freeman, 3 T.R. 51 (K.B. 1789).

[23] NLRA § 8(b)(7) prohibits picketing under specified circumstances "where an object thereof is forcing or requiring an employer to recognize or bargain with a labor organization as the representative of his employees, or forcing or requiring the employees of an employer to accept or select such labor organization as their collective bargaining representative."

[24] *E.g.*, Hall Freight Lines, Inc., 65 N.L.R.B. 397 (1946).

Banning organizational picketing after an NLRB election also partially rejects Holmes' philosophy of the free struggle for life,[25] for it prefers the nonunion employees' interest in self-determination over the union's interest in spreading its organization as a means of protecting its wage scale and labor standards. Suppose, however, that a union were to picket for the avowed purpose of publicizing the low wages paid in an establishment, without becoming the bargaining representative, in order to compel the owner to raise his wages to the union scale or else to prevent the distribution of low-cost nonunion goods in direct competition with the products of union labor. Section 8(b)(7) of the NLRA prohibits picketing only "where an object thereof is forcing or requiring an employer to recognize or bargain with a labor organization as the representative of his employees or . . . the employees of an employer to accept or select such labor organization as their collective bargaining representative. . . ."

The very few men close to the drafting of the Conference Report who understood this problem had no common intention—perhaps "had conflicting intentions" would be a better phrase. Presumably the NLRB will follow the decisions under Section 8(b)(4)(C) in which it announced a rule that picketing in support of a demand which is customarily made in collective bargaining is picketing for recognition.[26] I am inclined to think that the rule is wrong in principle, and it is opposed by judicial rulings distinguishing organizational picketing from picketing to protest the competition of nonunion goods.[27] The prohibition seeks to protect the employees' decision concerning union representation, not their freedom to work at substandard wages without reprisal from those whom they injure. The union's objective of eliminating the competition based upon differences in labor standards can be accomplished without interfering with the employees' decision concerning union representation. There is some risk that this approach would encourage the kind of verbal evasion which I criticized earlier, but the danger can be

[25] See p. 5 *supra*.

[26] Teamsters Local 626, 115 N.L.R.B. 890 (1956); International Ass'n of Machinists, District 24 (Industrial Chrome Plating Co.), 121 N.L.R.B. 1298 (1958). Although a broader rule was declared, the cases can be limited on their facts to holdings that § 8(b)(4)(C) applies unless the evidence permits a finding of fact that the union was *not* seeking recognition. In both cases there was reason to believe that *in fact* recognition was the demand.

[27] International Bhd. of Carpenters, Local 857 v. Todd L. Storms Constr. Co., 84 Ariz. 120, 329 P.2d 1002 (1958); Standard Grocer Co. v. Local No. 406, International Bhd. of Teamsters, 321 Mich. 276, 32 N.W.2d 519 (1948); cf. Douds v. Knit Goods Workers, Local 155, 147 F. Supp. 345 (E.D.N.Y. 1957); Starr v. Cooks, Waiters, Waitresses and Helpers Union, Local 458, 244 Minn. 558, 70 N.W.2d 873 (1955).

eliminated by treating the union's objective as a question of fact which requires looking behind the ostensible purpose. Regardless of what the union may say, recognition is an objective of any picketing of an unorganized shop, but the force of this presumption, based upon experience, can be dissipated by proof that the labor conditions of which the union complains present such an immediate and substantial threat to existing union standards in other shops, through the force of competition, as to support a finding that the union has a genuine interest in compelling the improvement of the labor conditions or eliminating the competition even though it does not become the bargaining representative.

Picketing before a union election is divided by Section 8(b)(7) into two categories: (i) picketing which halts pickups or deliveries by independent trucking concerns or the rendition of services by the employees of other employers, and (ii) picketing which appeals only to employees in the establishment and members of the public. The distinction is in terms of consequences rather than intent because motives are too difficult to disentangle. The theory is that the former class of picketing is essentially a signal to organized economic action backed by group discipline. Such economic pressure, if continued, causes heavy loss and increases the likelihood of the employer's coercing the employees to join the union. In the second type of picketing the elements of communication predominate. If the employer loses patronage, it is chiefly because of the impact of the picket's message upon members of the public acting as individuals.[28] The NLRB, in administering Section 8(b)(7), should recognize that it draws a line between two courses of conduct. Proof of a few widely separated refusals to cross a publicity picket line should not convert it into signal picketing.

Congress placed no limitation upon the period for which a union may engage in publicity picketing.[29] Signal picketing is treated as a legitimate organizing tactic until the election has been held, but in order to prevent the union from avoiding an election by disclaiming,

[28] This distinction between "signal picketing" and "publicity picketing" has been noted in discussions of the question whether picketing should be protected by the First and Fourteenth Amendments as a method of communication, but it attracted no significant judicial support. See Traynor, J., dissenting in Hughes v. Superior Court, 32 Cal.2d 850, 871, 198 P.2d 885, 897–898 (1948); Cox, *Strikes, Picketing and the Constitution,* 4 VAND. L. REV. 574, 591–597 (1951).

[29] This point may be open to debate although the sense seems clear. The second proviso makes it plain that § 8(b)(7)(C) does not apply to publicity picketing. It does apply to signal picketing, which is made unlawful after thirty days unless a petition for an election is filed. The words "such petition" in the first proviso refer only to a

or avoiding a claim of, representation rights, Section 8(b)(7)(D) prohibits signal picketing for more than a reasonable period, not to exceed thirty days, without filing a petition, upon which the NLRB is to proceed forthwith to an election. The signal picketing may then continue until the election is held. After the election all picketing, signal or publicity, is forbidden for reasons explained above.

Under the *Curtis Bros.*[80] and *Alloy*[81] doctrines the NLRB interpreted Section 8(b)(1) to impose some restrictions upon organizational activities which are more severe than Section 8(b)(7). Its decision in the *Alloy* case, for example, forbids organizing a consumer boycott after an election even though there is no picketing, whereas Section 8(b)(7) forbids only picketing. In other instances Section 8(b)(7) is the more restrictive. The final sentence of Section 8(b)(7) reads: "Nothing in this paragraph (7) shall be construed to permit any act which would otherwise be an unfair labor practice under section 8(b)." Does this mean that the soundness of the *Curtis* and *Alloy* doctrines must be decided under Section 8(b)(1) as if Section 8(b)(7) had not been enacted? Although the quoted words will bear this meaning, after Congress sharply debated the entire question and expressed its conclusions in Section 8(b)(7) it would seem wrong to construe the vague words of Section 8(b)(1) as a license for further administrative or judicial restrictions upon the use of concerted activities as organizing weapons.

The Statement of the Managers on the part of the House reads: "Section 8(b)(7) overrules the *Curtis* and *Alloy* cases to the extent that those decisions are inconsistent with section 8(b)(7)."[32] No citations were included. If the reference to the *Curtis* and *Alloy* cases directs attention to the NLRB decisions, the statement supports the argument that their more restrictive aspects survive. However, since the circuit courts had reversed the NLRB, the statement may be explaining that the court decisions are overruled to the extent that Section 8(b)(7) forbids organizational picketing.

---

petition filed to satisfy the requirement of § 8(b)(7)(C), *i.e.*, while there is signal picketing. To read the first proviso as if it meant a petition for an election filed while publicity is going on would defeat the whole purpose of the second proviso, which is obviously intended to secure the privilege of using publicity in order to obtain recognition, if there is no other representative.

[80] 119 N.L.R.B. 232 (1957), *rev'd*, 43 L.R.R.M. 2156 (D.C. Cir. 1958), *cert. granted*, 359 U.S. 965 (1959).

[81] International Ass'n of Machinists, Lodge 942, 119 N.L.R.B. 307 (1957), *enforced in part and set aside in part*, 263 F.2d 796 (9th Cir. 1959), *petition for cert. filed*, 28 U.S.L. Week 3011 (U.S. Apr. 24, 1959) (No. 57).

[82] 105 CONG. REC. 16552 (daily ed. Sept. 3, 1959).

It may clarify the situation to recount the pertinent events. The conferees did not overlook the ambiguous sentence. On the part of the Senate the fear was expressed that the sentence might keep alive the litigation over the *Curtis* and *Alloy* doctrines and thus lead to judicial and administrative restrictions in addition to those imposed by Section 8(b)(7). Proponents of the Landrum-Griffin bill disclaimed this intent, but they were unwilling to delete the sentence for fear that the deletion might somehow be construed to imply that Section 8(b)(7) qualified Section 8(b)(4) or other unfair labor practices having nothing to do with the use of picketing or other publicity in an organizing campaign. The difference was resolved by the suggestion that the House Managers should include the following statement in their explanation of the conference agreement:

> The final sentence in proposed section 8(b)(7) is intended to make it clear that section 8(b)(7) does not qualify any of the other unfair labor practices under section 8(b). Section 8(b)(7) is, of course, intended as a definitive legislative disposition of the problems involved in the *Curtis* and *Alloy* cases.

This passage was mimeographed in a sheet containing two similar passages comprising other issues, distributed and read aloud at a later meeting of conferees with the staff present, and approved without dissent. The Statement of the House Managers had not been prepared when the Senate voted. It was not shown to the Senate staff. Instead of the agreed explanation it contains the sentence quoted above. The sense would be the same if the actual statement means that the court decisions in the *Curtis* and *Alloy* cases are overruled where inconsistent with Section 8(b)(7).

In summary, the present law of organizational picketing compromises conflicting interests. Signal picketing is an economic weapon which may seriously injure an employer's business and exert sufficient economic pressure upon the employees to coerce their choice of representatives. It can be argued that such a method of organizing is unnecessary and inappropriate today because the NLRA prevents coercion by employers. On the other hand, the union members have an important economic interest in protecting their wages and working conditions. The protection against employer interference available under the NLRA is imperfect because of the delays and uncertainties of litigation, the manifold opportunities for subtle discrimination, and the coercion exercised through freedom of expression. Since all unionization involves a revolution against the established order, picketing affords a demonstration that there is another power factor in the situation, which may be essential to spark the revolt. An election is the only truly reliable test of employee sentiment; until it is held one cannot be sure that the pickets do not speak for the majority. The relative weights to be assigned to these considerations vary from case to case—there are instances in which two days of organizational picketing would destroy a business and others in which two months of picketing would be beneficent—yet the necessary appraisals are too particularized for practical administration. One's final judgment must depend partly upon the degree of his reluctance to curtail a weapon of self-advancement and partly upon his appraisal of the value of further unionization. In my opinion Section 8(b)(7) strikes as fair a balance as has yet been suggested, provided that the inadequacies of the draftsmanship are corrected by understanding administration.[38]

II

In public and congressional debate a "secondary boycott" is something very bad, but just what it is, and why it is bad, are seldom stated. Historically a boycott is a refusal to have dealings with an offending person. To induce customers not to buy from an offending grocery store is to organize a primary boycott. To persuade grocery stores not to buy Swift products is still a primary boycott. In each case the only economic pressure is leveled at the offending person—in terms of labor cases, at the employer involved in the labor dispute.

The element of "secondary activity" is introduced when there is a refusal to have dealings with one who has dealings with the offending person. There is a secondary boycott if housewives refuse to buy at any grocery store which deals with Swift & Co. It is also a secondary boycott for members of the Plumbers Union to refuse to work for any contractor who buys pipe from U. S. Pipe Co. All true secondary boycotts involve two employers. The union brings pressure upon the employer with whom it has a dispute (called the "primary employer") by inducing the employees of other employers who deal with him (called the "secondary employers") to go on strike—or their customers not to patronize—until the secondary employers stop dealing with the primary employer. Or the union may simply induce the employees of a secondary employer to refuse to handle or work on goods—or the customers not to buy goods—coming from the primary employer while they perform the rest of their duties.

[38] No criticism of the author of the Landrum-Griffin bill is intended. The drafting was done under very difficult circumstances, and I have a share in the responsibility for mistakes.

Although the National Labor Relations Act does not use the words "primary boycott" or "secondary boycott," the distinction has an important influence upon both the drafting and interpretation of legislation. The differentiation is critical in dealing with picketing at the scene of a labor dispute. Suppose, for example, that the Teamsters Union induced the employees of the ABC Express Co. to refuse to transport furniture delivered at the ABC terminal by the Modern Furniture Co. some of whose employees are on strike. The inducement would have been a violation of Section 8(b)(4)(A) even before the Landrum-Griffin amendments because that section forbade a union (i.e., the Teamsters)

> to encourage the employees of any employer [i.e., the employees of ABC Express Co.] to engage in . . . a concerted refusal in the course of their employment to . . . handle or work on any goods . . . or to perform any services;. . . where . . . an object thereof is: . . . forcing or requiring any person to cease using, selling, handling, transporting, or otherwise dealing in the products of any other producer, processor, or manufacturer, or to cease doing business with any other person [i.e., Modern Furniture Co.].

Suppose now that the furniture company telephones the ABC Express Co. to pick up the furniture at the factory and that the strikers dissuade the express company's drivers from entering. The refusal to cross the picket line, not the strike, brings the economic pressure. The words of Section 8(b)(4)(A) are as applicable as in the first case, but the NLRB and court decisions under the Taft-Hartley Act hold that there is no violation chiefly because turning people away from the scene of a labor dispute is an incident of a primary strike rather than a secondary boycott.[34] The Supreme Court adopted this interpretation in the *Rice Milling* case,[35] but the opinion stressed the point that Section 8(b)(4)(A) prohibited inducements to engage in a "concerted refusal."[36] Since the Landrum-Griffin bill deleted this phrase, it might have overturned the entire line of decisions if a majority of the Senate conferees had not secured the inclusion of explicit language safeguarding the right to engage in primary picketing even though truck drivers are stopped by the pickets.[37]

[34] *E.g.*, Oil Workers Int'l Union, Local 346 (Pure Oil Co.), 84 N.L.R.B. 315 (1949); Moore Dry Dock Co., 92 N.L.R.B. 547 (1951); Columbia Southern Corp., 110 N.L.R.B. 206 (1954).

[35] NLRB v. International Rice Milling Co., 341 U.S. 665 (1951).

[36] 341 U.S. at 670.

[37] NLRA § 8(b)(4)(B), as amended, has a proviso reading: ". . . nothing contained in this clause (B) shall be construed to make unlawful, where not otherwise unlawful, any primary strike or primary picketing."

We shall return to this distinction in a moment but first suppose that prior to the strike at Modern Furniture Co. the Teamsters Union induced all the trucking concerns in the area to agree that they would not require their employees to handle the goods of an employer engaged in a labor dispute. Would it now be an unfair labor practice for the Teamsters Union to induce the express company's employees to refuse to handle the furniture? For six or seven years these "hot cargo" contracts were held to legitimatize the secondary boycott,[38] but in 1957 the Supreme Court held that the clause was not a defense.[39] However, if the trucker performed his promise voluntarily without the Teamsters inducing his employees not to work, there would be only a primary boycott and no violation of the Taft-Hartley Act.[40]

This was an impractical distinction. The effect upon the furniture company is the same as when the union induces the trucker's employees to refuse to handle the furniture. Furthermore, one wonders about the trucker's "voluntary" participation in the primary boycott. Would he sign the "hot cargo" clause without pressure from the Teamsters? Would he perform it but for the fear that if he fails the Teamsters will be tougher in the next contract negotiations or will remind him of his failure to perform his part of the contract whenever he asks the union to halt a wildcat strike? The only way of dealing with such pressures is to nip them in the bud by prohibiting the agreement. Apart from the participation of the labor union, even as primary boycotts they would violate the Sherman Act.[41]

This was the theory upon which the Senate voted to outlaw "hot cargo" contracts in the trucking industry. The words literally covered only an agreement by an employer that he would not handle the "hot cargo,"[42] but since a business firm acts through its employees, the prohibition would seem to extend to any promise not to require employees to handle the "hot cargo" or not to discipline employees for their

[38] International Bhd. of Teamsters, 87 N.L.R.B. 972 (1949), *aff'd,* 195 F.2d 906 (2d Cir. 1952).

[39] Local 1976, United Brotherhood of Carpenters v. NLRB, 357 U.S. 93 (1958).

[40] Section 8(b)(4)(A) prohibited only inducement of "employees."

[41] Fashion Originators' Guild v. Federal Trade Commission, 312 U.S. 457 (1941).

[42] Section 707 of S. 1555, as passed by the Senate, would have amended the NLRA by adding: "It shall be an unfair labor practice for any labor organization and any employer who is a common carrier subject to Part II of the Interstate Commerce Act to enter into any contract or agreement, express or implied, whereby such employer ceases or refrains or agrees to cease or refrain from handling, using, or transporting any of the products of any other employer, or to cease doing business with any other person."

refusal. In the House the prohibition was extended to all agreements by which an employer agrees with a labor organization not to handle or use the goods of another person,[43] but the rationale was not changed and this should dissipate organized labor's fears that the prohibition invalidates agreements sanctioning refusal to cross a primary picket line, such as the refusal of the truck drivers to cross the picket line at our hypothetical Modern Furniture plant. Thus, although Section 8(b)(4)(i)(B) speaks of all inducement of an employee of a secondary employer with an object of forcing him "to cease using, selling, handling, transporting or otherwise dealing in the products of any other producer, processor or manufacturer, or to cease doing business with any other person," under the *Rice Milling* case and the new confirmatory proviso explained above it is not an unlawful secondary boycott to induce employees to refuse to cross a primary picket line where the refusal causes the secondary employer to cease doing business with the primary employer *at the site of the labor dispute*. The same words are repeated in outlawing "hot cargo" agreements. The prohibition was drafted in aid of the restriction upon secondary boycotts. The same distinction based upon the situs should therefore be observed, with the result that Section 8(e) does not prohibit agreements sanctioning refusal to cross a lawful, primary picket line.

Although the language again leaves doubt, the underlying rationale should also exclude from Section 8(e) conventional restrictions upon subcontracting, such as the promise that "All work that is usually performed in the plants of the Company shall continue to be performed in such plants unless a change is mutually agreed upon by both parties."[44] In a literal sense this clause is an agreement between an employer and a union by which the employer undertakes not to do business with any other person, but it has a different function than the contracts which were the targets of Section 8(e). This restriction upon subcontracting seeks to protect the wages and job opportunities of the employees covered by the contract by forbidding the primary employer to have work which his employees might do, performed outside his own shop—something quite different in both purpose and effect from arranging to have secondary employers boycott nonunion firms or specified employers or groups of employers because their products or labor policies are objectionable to the union. The fact that Congress rejected

[43] NLRA § 8(e).

[44] Agreement between Selby Shoe Co. and United Shoe Workers of America, Local 117, effective November 11, 1947.

the attacks upon the secondary boycott provisions of the Landrum-Griffin bill alleging that it unwisely threw doubt upon the validity of bona fide restrictions upon subcontracting may be attributed to disbelief in the allegation just as easily as to congressional opposition to contractual restrictions upon managerial freedom to subcontract, although there were undoubtedly individuals who hoped also to resolve the subcontracting issue in favor of management. Whatever the merits of the latter issue, it is distinct from the only explicit subject of legislative concern.

The prohibition of "hot cargo" contracts is the most vulnerable of the Landrum-Griffin amendments. In the trucking industry it will serve a useful purpose. The construction and apparel and clothing industries were excepted because the prohibition would have wreaked havoc. Congress had no information about the prevalence or uses of similar clauses in other industries, about their impact upon employers or their importance to union organization. The majority in the House of Representatives was content to make the loose assumption that a clause which was against public policy in the transportation industry must be equally undesirable in other segments of the economy. The Senate conferees could not induce them to change.

Perhaps we have also erred in treating all secondary boycotts alike. The external conduct is simply a concerted refusal to work set in motion by picketing or some equivalent inducement by union leaders. Since the conduct is not morally wrong and invades no immediate personal or property right, there is no reason for forbidding it unless the social or economic consequences are judged unfair or undesirable. Formulating such a judgment would seem to call for an examination of all the consequences, yet the statute makes the involvement of a secondary employer the sole criterion upon the theory that he is a neutral bystander whom it is unfair to subject to intentional economic loss in a quarrel not of his making.

The criterion falls demonstrably short of accomplishing perfect justice. The neutrality of the secondary employer varies within such wide limits that the courts have already read two exceptions into the statute which the Landrum-Griffin amendments impliedly retain. Royal Typewriter Co. maintains business machines leased to its customers. During a strike Royal's employees refused to do the maintenance work, and the company arranged to have other concerns perform the contracts with their employees for the account of Royal. The union thereupon induced the employees employed by the independent repair shops to refuse to do the strikers' work. The union's conduct violated the literal meaning of Section 8(b)(4)(A), but the Court of Appeals for the Second Circuit held that there was no unfair labor practice because the secondary employer had interjected himself into the dispute as the ally of the primary employer.[45]

The second judge-made exception involves corporate affiliates. The wholly owned subsidiary of a whiskey distiller would not be treated as a disinterested neutral in a dispute at the distillery. The common ownership plus the assistance which the distributor gives the distiller by selling its products, and only its products, shows that they share a common goal and common interests.[46]

Picketing a nonunion contractor on a construction project is held to be an unlawful secondary boycott because it induces the employees of the other contractors to quit work.[47] The situation is distinguishable from the *Royal Typewriter* and corporate affiliate cases but the difference is only in degree. All the employers affected by picketing of a construction project are bound together in the common work. None is completely neutral since the undertaking is integral. Each is affected by, and can influence, the conduct of the others.

One seeking perfect justice in an individual case would consider three other factors which are irrelevant under Section 8(b)(4)(A). The interest of the secondary employees in the outcome of the dispute is significant. Where all the men are employed in the same industry and in the same locality, as in the case of a construction job, the division into different trades or crafts, each with its own employer, cannot obscure their common interests—they work side by side and the wages and working conditions of one trade affect all the others. Quite the reverse is true of other secondary boycotts; the outcome of a wage dispute in a Minnesota woodworking factory will not affect the wages of construction carpenters in Los Angeles.

The purpose of the boycott is highly important. In the *Bedford Stone Cutters* case,[48] which a generation of students studied as proof of the unfairness of labor injunctions, the union was struggling to preserve its existence in the face of a lockout and company-dominated union. At

---

[45] NLRB v. Business Mach. & Office Appliance Mechanics Conference Bd., Local 459, 228 F.2d 553 (2d Cir. 1955). The Statement of the House Managers explicitly approved this interpretation. H.R. Rep. No. 1147, 86th Cong., 1st Sess. 38 (1959).

[46] *Accord,* J. G. Roy and Sons Co. v. NLRB, 251 F.2d 771 (1st Cir. 1958).

[47] NLRB v. Denver Bldg. & Constr. Trades Council, 341 U.S. 675 (1951).

[48] Bedford Cut Stone Co. v. Journeymen Stone Cutters Ass'n., 274 U.S. 37 (1927).

the other end of the range lies the notorious boycott sponsored by Local 3 of the International Brotherhood of Electrical Workers during the course of which the electricians on construction work refused to install electrical equipment which had not been manufactured by members of Local 3, a requirement which excluded all out-of-city manufacturers from the New York market, thereby swelling the coffers of the New York concerns and enabling them to pay higher wages.[49] Local 3's trade barrier has current parallels in contracts negotiated by the United Association of Journeymen Plumbers which require plumbing contractors to install only pipe fabricated by union members.

A third factor in any pragmatic evaluation of a particular secondary boycott would be the power and necessities of the labor union which organized the boycott. An unrestricted right to engage in secondary boycotts would give the Teamsters Union overwhelming power through its grasp upon the bottleneck of transportation. The building trades unions, which have organized 80 per cent of the construction industry, made frequent use of the secondary boycott against "unfair" materials prior to the Taft-Hartley Act. None of these organizations needs additional bargaining power. In the apparel and clothing industry, on the other hand, the boycott is probably essential to effective collective bargaining. In the early days whenever the International Ladies' Garment Workers established a wage scale and working conditions, employers would circumvent the contract by subcontracting cutting, sewing, or other operations to a nonunion establishment. The jobber whose costs were rising because his contractors observed union standards came under competitive pressure to take work away from union contractors and give it to sweatshops. The union could never catch up with all the nonunion contractors because their operations did not require a heavy capital investment and the equipment could easily be moved from one loft to another. The number of jobbers, however, is relatively small. The International Ladies' Garment Workers became capable of maintaining its organization and establishing better conditions of employment when it began to negotiate contracts with jobbers restricting their choice of subcontractors to firms which maintained union conditions of employment.

The foregoing factors seem plainly relevant to any impartial appraisal of the effect of a secondary boycott upon both the immediate parties and the community, yet the present law requires the NLRB to disregard them. One alternative would be to allow the NLRB or the courts to evaluate the relevant factors in every case and declare

[49] Allen-Bradley Co. v. Local 3, IBEW, 325 U.S. 797 (1945).

judgment upon the balance; but this suggestion has several fatal defects. It overlooks the need for a fixed standard by which employers and labor unions can know their rights in projecting a course of conduct. It requires the use of particularized economic data which is hard to obtain and still more difficult to present in litigation without a lengthy and expensive trial. In the final analysis judgment would often turn upon the length of the chancellor's foot, for there is no magic scale of values by which one could assign points for the degree of the secondary employer's neutrality, the degree of his employees' interest in the primary dispute, the character of the objective, and the importance of the secondary boycott to the particular union as a method of employee self-help. Where the present law is excessively general, the alternative is excessively impractical; therefore neither is entirely just.

Perhaps there is a middle ground. The recent amendments modify the blanket prohibition in the case of the apparel and clothing industry because its special character was forcibly presented to the Conference Committee.[80] The courts created one exception for refusals to perform struck work and appear to be developing another for corporate affiliates. During the Landrum-Griffin debates congressional leaders in both parties promised to bring to the floor in 1960 legislation specially designed to permit the picketing of construction projects. Such straws in the wind suggest that the basic dilemma can be minimized by more careful statutory classification. Even today a few additional distinctions could be justified without further data. The use of boycotts to suppress competition between employers in the product market should be handled as a restraint of trade; both labor relations and the administration of antitrust laws are needlessly complicated when such boycotts are swept into the same category as efforts to organize nonunion competitors. The establishment of other appropriate categories waits upon adequate research, for convincing factual data are necessary to overcome the hostile public reaction aroused by the words "secondary boycott." The research should be directed toward developing classifications which can be administered by law. If it succeeded, the law of secondary boycotts could be brought more nearly into harmony with social and economic realities.

III

The need of labor unions for freedom to use picketing and boycotts as methods of achieving organization and collective bargaining depends in part upon the weapons available to employers in restricting the

[80] A proviso to NLRA § 8(e) excepts this industry from §§ 8(e) and 8(b)(4)(B).

unionization of their employees. The fundamental rights to organize and bargain collectively, created by the Railway Labor and Wagner Acts, are contested around their edges but the core is a permanent part of our labor law. The Taft-Hartley and Landrum-Griffin amendments did not change the basic statutory provisions creating employer unfair labor practices. The wisdom of legal protection for the hard core of rights is not open to serious public dispute.

But this is only part of the story. Under the Wagner Act the National Labor Relations Board was dominated by zeal, perhaps excessive zeal, for unionization. Today the Board, the General Counsel, and the staffs, who are as concerned with restraining union misconduct as employer unfair practices, conceive themselves to be arbitrators between individual employees, management, and union. The change is epitomized in the Taft-Hartley revision of Section 7, which currently places the rights not to organize, not to bargain collectively, and not to engage in concerted activities upon a parity with the original rights to engage in such activities. It appears to have been the result of a widespread public belief that labor unions had become so strong that legislative action was required to redress the balance of power. The power of unions already organized might logically justify strengthening the employer's hand in collective bargaining and even curtailing the strong union's right to use economic weapons to organize nonunion shops, but it has no proper place in formulating or administering public policy toward employers' interference with organizational activities among unorganized employees. The power of the United Automobile Workers *vis-à-vis* employers in the automotive industry is logically irrelevant to the Textile Workers' efforts to organize southern textile mills. The Taft-Hartley and Landrum-Griffin restrictions upon boycotts and picketing require increased protection against interference, coercion, and restraint of employees in the exercise of the right of self-organization.

These are distinctions with which the law can deal. The failure to make them is testimony to the irrationality of the legislative process in debating labor legislation. Since the enactment of any labor legislation apparently depends upon broad swings in the pendulum of public sentiment, it may be hard for the legislator to follow the course of reason and support measures strengthening unions during the organizational phase of labor relations while controlling unions with established power. Surely we were entitled to expect a greater capacity for differentiation from the executive branch and the National Labor Relations Board.

They have not made the differentiations. The basic shift from a policy of encouraging unionization to one of indifference is reflected in the NLRB attitude toward the active opposition of employers to union organization. Prior to 1947, and in some degree from 1947 to 1953, the Board's premise was that the employer, though he might be opposed to unions, had no legally cognizable interest in preventing the unionization of his plant. Since many specific issues arising in the administration of the Act turn upon the balance of conflicting interests, assigning a zero value to the employer's interest in breaking up an incipient union would frequently tip the scale in the union's favor. A case in point is the former rule that interrogation of employees concerning union activities is an unfair labor practice per se,[51] for although the degree of coercion may be very slight, the employer rarely has enough legitimate interest in the information to justify even the slight interference with freedom to organize. Since 1953 a majority of the NLRB members appear to have followed a philosophy set forth during the Taft-Hartley debates by an employer's attorney who later became Solicitor of the Department of Commerce:

> [W]e hear much said about employers "intimidating" employees. We forget that the employee is now under the system of unions which has been created by patronage of Government somewhat in the position of a customer about to buy an article with both the union and the employer competing for his allegiance, trade and support.[52]

Under this view the function of the NLRB is to establish the Marquis of Queensbury rules defining the weapons with which employers and unions wage the contest over unionization. The interrogation of employees is now held not to be unlawful per se.[53]

Of course, it is the application of general views of policy to concrete cases which has practical importance, and in a real sense a policy is derived from its specific applications. The attitude which I criticize appears in many rulings upon issues which in isolation have no great importance and may even appear to be nicely balanced, but the cumulative disposition of which encourages or checks the spread of collective bargaining.

An excellent example is the change in NLRB rules concerning an employer's refusal to bargain with a new union. Under the statute two courses of action are open. The first is to charge the employer with the

[51] Standard-Coosa-Thatcher Co., 85 N.L.R.B. 1358 (1949), expressly overruled by Blue Flash Express, Inc., 109 N.L.R.B. 591 (1954).

[52] *Hearings on S. 55 Before Senate Committee on Labor and Public Welfare,* 80th Cong., 1st Sess. 1700 (1947).

[53] Blue Flash Express, Inc., 109 N.L.R.B. 591 (1954).

unfair labor practice of refusing to bargain collectively with the representatives designated by a majority of the employees in an appropriate unit, in violation of Section 8(a)(5). The case would be made out if it were proved at the hearing that the unit claimed was appropriate, that a majority of the employees in the unit supported the union on the day it requested recognition, and that the employer nevertheless refused to bargain.[54] The alternative course of action is to have an election whenever the employer's refusal to bargain is accompanied by a request that the union prove its majority.

The latter course has much to commend it. An election is the most reliable test of employee sentiment. Since a finding concerning the employees' wishes on the date of the employer's refusal to bargain may depend upon inference or conflicting evidence, there is often substantial risk of making an erroneous finding which would fasten an unwanted representative upon both employees and employer. Furthermore, since an employer who has a bona fide and reasonable doubt concerning the union's status ought not to be prosecuted for an unfair labor practice, a decision to proceed under Section 8(a)(5) involves investigation of an uncertain state of mind. All these dangers would be avoided by adopting the hard and fast rule of thumb that the NLRB would never find an employer guilty of a violation of Section 8(a)(5) because of his refusal to bargain without an NLRB election. The rule would also give the NLRB staff a simple set of instructions which dispensed with both the need for investigation and the responsibility for passing judgment.

But consider the effect upon union organization. Union organizers frequently find it difficult to keep up enthusiasm in a new local without producing results as well as promises. In a contested case—and the employer can always raise a contest—it takes from six months to a year for the NLRB to hold an election. The new union is made to appear inept and futile; apparently it can accomplish nothing, but meanwhile the employer may bring pressure upon the employees through antiunion propaganda and the community may array itself in opposition through the police, the mayor, the churches, and the chamber of commerce. Unfair labor practice proceedings are also time-consuming, but if the employer is found guilty, the NLRB restores the status quo by directing him to bargain with the union without regard

[54] NLRA §§ 8(a)(5) and 9(a) do not condition the employer's duty to bargain upon an NLRB certification.

to subsequent changes in employee sentiment, thereby depriving the employer of the fruits of misconduct.[55] For almost two decades the NLRB proceeded under Section 8(a)(5) when there was evidence that the employer's request for an election was not the result of a bona fide doubt concerning the union's status; in 1954 this avenue was closed and elections were required whenever the employer requested the union to prove its majority unless there was evidence that the employer had used the delay to commit flagrant unfair labor practices undermining the union's strength.[56]

The new practice is obviously based upon a re-evaluation of the public interest in protecting union organization and collective bargaining, which subordinates it to the competing interests mentioned above. The new rule is not unreasonable. Some risk has to be taken whichever route is followed. The vice is that the change in policy typifies a whole series of shifts in NLRB rules of decision each of which puts more risks upon the unions, with the result that their cumulative impact makes it immensely more difficult to organize nonunion establishments.

NLRB rulings upon employers' antiunion speeches furnish another example. Freedom of expression ranks high in our scale of values; its curtailment can be justified only by strong necessity. Most of us also value full freedom for employees in forming, joining, and assisting labor organizations of their own choosing. To pursue either goal to its logical extreme requires some sacrifice of the other. Arguments which disclose the speaker's strong desire are not wholly an appeal to reason if the listener is in the speaker's power. As Judge Learned Hand pointed out:

> Words . . . take their purport from the setting in which they are used, of which the relation between the speaker and the hearer is perhaps the most important part. What to an outsider will be no more than the vigorous presentation of a conviction, to an employee may be the manifestation of a determination which it is not safe to thwart.[57]

Judging whether the coercive elements in an employer's verbal attack upon a union outweigh its value as argumentation cannot be wholly divorced from one's intuitive appraisal of the relative values of freedom of association and freedom of expression. The lower value which the NLRB now puts upon freedom of association and the notion that an employer has a legitimate interest in defeating a union have led

[55] Franks Bros. Co. v. NLRB, 321 U.S. 702 (1944).
[56] The leading case is A. L. Gilbert Co., 110 N.L.R.B. 2067 (1954).
[57] L. Hand, J., in NLRB v. Federbush Co., 121 F.2d 954, 957 (2d Cir. 1941).

to increasing the latitude allowed employers in the name of free speech to the point where a clever lawyer can readily show an employer how to threaten and coerce his employees without fear of NLRB proceedings. An employer may not lawfully "threaten" to reduce wages or close a plant if a union is organized but he may "predict" that these things will happen. In *Chicopee Mfg. Co.*,[58] a company which owned several textile plants told the employees at one plant just before an election that the company could not afford to pay the union wage scale at the plant in question, that the management "could move the plant if they so desired," and that "if the union won they would be forced to move the plant." These statements were held to be permissible predictions, but surely the employees had no doubt of the threat implied. Similarly, an employer may not lawfully threaten to refuse to bargain with a union but he may state his legal position. In *National Furniture Mfg. Co.*[59] it was held that there was no threat in asserting that "it would not make any difference whether the union won the election or not; the Company would not recognize it." The most amusing illustration is an unreported case which arose in one of the New England fishing ports. Just before an election the employer posted a notice in one of its processing plants, saying in substance:

> The management has diverted the S.S. Cape Ann to another plant in Boston because it cannot afford to bring additional fish to this plant until the threat of labor unrest is removed.

The employees took the hint and voted against the union; but the election was set aside because the notice was threatening. Later a new election was held. Two days before the new election the employer posted a notice the gist of which was:

> You may wonder why a new election is being held so soon after the union was soundly beaten in a prior election. The explanation is that the first election was set aside by the NLRB because the company posted the following notice of management policy just prior to the election:

Then followed the earlier notice. This time the ruling was that management had done nothing more than explain the legal situation.

In criticizing the NLRB rulings I do not mean to suggest a return to the much earlier rule by which employers were forbidden to express themselves in opposition to labor unions. No change in the statute is necessary although its revision might usefully symbolize dissatisfaction with the course of decision. The fault lies in the failure to give effect

[58] 107 N.L.R.B. 106 (1956).
[59] 106 N.L.R.B. 1300 (1953).

to the simple truth that the impact of the words is a function of the time and place, of the positions of the speaker and listener, of the tone and past relations—in short, of environment and experience. Words which may only antagonize a hard-bitten truck driver in Detroit may seriously intimidate a rural textile hand in a company village where the mill owners dominate every aspect of life. The dictionary meaning is irrelevant; the question is, what did the speaker intend and the listener understand. This approach to free speech cases would take the decision out of the hands of review attorneys sitting in Washington and vest it in the trial examiners who absorb the atmosphere by visiting the community and observing the parties and witnesses. It might even substitute for neat little agency rules based upon verbalisms the kind of intuitive reaction which influences a jury; mistakes would result but on the whole greater justice would be done.

Before leaving this aspect of the subject we should consider one other form of interference with freedom of association. Efforts to extend union organization in the South frequently encounter community opposition. In Porterdale, Georgia, for example, the Bibb Manufacturing Co. owned all the property except the churches, and supplied all the utilities and public services except police protection. All the town officials were Bibb's employees. When the Textile Workers Union sought to organize the mill, uniformed police officers openly followed each union organizer wherever he went and whatever he did for twenty-four hours a day. Not many employees would be ready to exercise the right to join the union and take part in its activities under these conditions. In Orangeburg, South Carolina, the chamber of commerce sent a letter to each employee of the Southland Provision Co. just before an NLRB election containing arguments about the harm done to the community by labor unions and concluding:

> The merchants and citizens of Orangeburg feel that those who help run industry away from Orangeburg and who cause Orangeburg to lose the benefits of large payrolls should not be given any special privileges in the future in the way of job preference, credit, etc.
>
> For this reason if you are not active for the union please notify us so that we will not do you the injustice of putting your name on the blacklist.

Such activities unquestionably restrain and coerce employees in the exercise of the right to self-organization, but they cannot be prevented under the present law unless the employer authorized or ratified them.[60] Union propagandists blame the rule on the Taft-Hartley amendments

[60] NLRA §§ 2(2) and (13).

because the original NLRA held the employer responsible for the conduct of persons acting in his interest whereas the revised version imputes to him only the acts of his agents,[61] but proof of some connection between the employer and the coercion has always been required;[62] unfortunately the evidence is seldom available in this class of cases. To assert that the employer must be to blame whether proof is available or not, is to overlook the depth of community feeling and substitute antagonism for evidence.

The NLRA might be amended so as to prohibit interference, coercion, or restraint from any source, but this would involve a major departure from the traditions of Anglo-American law. No government agency has general jurisdiction to investigate and redress private interference with freedom of speech, political activity, or religion. Freedom to organize labor unions has no stronger claim to protection. Under these circumstances it seems unlikely that the NLRB will be given general authority to deal with interference with freedom to form, join, and assist labor organizations. A new, more imaginative solution must be found.

IV

The weakening of government protection for union organization was not necessary to prevent the abuse of power by strong unions or to carry out the logical implications of the National Labor Relations Act. Some restrictions upon picketing and secondary boycotts were required, but in the latter case, at least, they could have been applied with a nicer sense of discrimination. Proof is hard to find because we lack the control needed for purposes of comparison, but there seems little ground for doubting the importance of these changes in checking the spread of union organization.

Yet those of us who deplore the changes because we believe that labor unions are essential to freedom and democracy in an industrial society must guard against exaggerating the blame to be laid upon public policy for the present low estate of the labor movement. Other

[61] *E.g.*, Wyle, *Union Organization Activity Under Taft-Hartley*, N.Y.U. 11th Ann. Conf. on Labor 191, 211–217 (1958).

[62] In Salant & Salant, Inc., 66 N.L.R.B. 24 (1946), a case which is often cited to demonstrate the supposed breadth of the pre-Taft-Hartley Act rule, the Board found that the citizens' committees were organized and stimulated by the employer. A little later the same concern was held not to be responsible for the antiunion activities of town officials unless they could be connected to the company. Salant & Salant, Inc., 87 N.L.R.B. 215, 225 (1949). See also NLRB v. American Pearl Button Co., 149 F.2d 311 (8th Cir. 1945); NLRB v. Mylan-Sparta Co., 166 F.2d 485 (6th Cir. 1948).

external and internal forces have been at work. They partially explain both the changes in public policy and the failure of unions to add new members.

The slower expansion of union membership can be partly explained by the changing frontiers of union organization. Although experience in the Scandinavian countries and upon our own Pacific Coast shows that white-collar workers can be organized, labor unions and collective bargaining are less necessary for, and less attractive to, employees in offices and service establishments than in large mines, mills, and factories. In the South union organizers confronted entire communities whose social and economic strata resisted unionization and whose leaders resorted to tactics which the industrial metropolises of the North and West would no longer tolerate. Law cannot force unions upon communities which are basically opposed; yet as industrialization of the South proceeds, surely national policy should encourage the spread of collective bargaining and prevent interference in the interest of employers.

Changes in management are also important. There is more organized opposition to unions, although the techniques are subtler, but there is also more disposition to remove the causes at the root of unionization.

The improvement in wages and conditions of labor which has occurred in the past quarter century would seem to be a third important factor explaining the reduced rate of growth. A general public which would ardently support the labor movement when the average hourly earnings of a steelworker were 66 cents an hour feels less enthusiasm now that they are $2.88 an hour with pensions and hospital and medical service in addition. In the automotive industry the average annual wage and salary payments for a full-time employee increased from $1,170 in 1933 to $1,762 in 1939 and $5,443 in 1956. The improved position of the industrial worker is both absolute and relative. While the annual wage and salary payments of the automobile worker were increasing almost fivefold and of the textile worker roughly fourfold, the consumers' price index little more than doubled. The annual wage and salary payments in finance, insurance, and real estate increased from $1,555 in 1933 to $1,729 in 1939 and $4,226 in 1956—less than a threefold increase compared with the fivefold increase of the automobile worker. Twenty-five years ago organized labor's demand for "more and more and more" evoked the sympathy of many idealists; not a few of them joined the ranks. Today the bloom is gone from the rose.

A fourth factor, which is certain to grow in importance, is the change in the character of the work force. The demand for skilled workers is constantly increasing. More and more wage earners are exchanging white collars for blue. It seems likely that a constantly smaller proportion of the population will be employed in the production and distribution of goods. We cannot foresee the total impact of electronics, of the peaceful use of atomic energy, and of the space age, but the vague outlines are enough to raise the question whether the new scientific revolutions may not outdate the institutions—labor unions and collective bargaining—which an earlier revolution made important.

I hope not. We cannot return to the individualistic American society of the seventeenth, eighteenth, and nineteenth centuries, but perhaps we can preserve the pluralism which permits fluidity of movement and diversity of thought, and thus gives scope for individual realization. In a pluralistic community there is need for labor unions if they can adapt themselves to change. Thus far they have done the job rather badly.

This brings us to my final thought. Are not the labor movement's failure to grow and the decline of its prestige partly attributable to its own loss of idealism? Many of the intellectuals who grew up under the New Deal may have allowed a romantic glow to obscure harsh facts, but I cannot believe that they were entirely wrong in sensing a vitality which had something quite different to offer than wealth and power for union officials and more and more monetary benefits for union members.

Chapter 3

The Role of Public Policy in the Negotiation of Collective Bargaining Agreements

The American system of industrial relations rests upon private enterprise in markets which, despite increasing government regulation, are still remarkably free. We believe in individual initiative, private decision-making, and personal responsibility not only as economic and political doctrine but also as moral philosophy, although our beliefs run beyond our practice in this respect as well as others. Organized labor is scarcely less committed to the existing system than other segments of the community. It attracts more idealists, reformers, and rebels, but most union officials, whether business agents or general presidents, have the same basic beliefs as their corporate counterparts. Specifically, they share the conviction that wages and conditions of employment must be fixed by private agreement.

Labor's acceptance of this postulate depends upon maintaining freedom to organize and bargain collectively, including the right to strike. Employees can influence negotiations in the labor market only by collective bargaining. One cannot negotiate without ability to reject the proffered terms. The only way in which employees can reject an employer's offer is to stop work. Consequently, collective bargaining can hardly exist without preserving the right to strike.

The role of labor relations law has been to provide a framework for this system. The Taft-Hartley Act prescribes a few procedural steps[1] and the National Labor Relations Board has undertaken not only to judge the conduct of the negotiators but also to determine what subjects the negotiators must cover.[2] These decisions contrast strangely with the utter lack of government policy upon such critical issues as wages and

[1] NLRA § 8(d). The requirements relate chiefly to the reopening or renewal of existing collective bargaining agreements.

[2] For detailed discussion of this point see Cox and Dunlop, *Regulation of Collective Bargaining by the National Labor Relations Board,* 63 HARV. L. REV. 389 (1950); COX, *Labor Decisions of the Supreme Court at the October Term, 1957,* 44 VA. L. REV. 1057, 1074–86 (1958).

automation and with the want of machinery for making a policy felt. The full extent of our commitment to governmental inaction is evidenced by the Taft-Hartley prohibition against even recommendations by a Board of Inquiry appointed to investigate a dispute which endangers the national health or safety. The central issue of labor policy today is whether the country should chart a new course.

1. *Can we not devise a better method of adjusting conflicts of interest between employers and employees in essential industries where a cessation of operations may create an imminent threat to the national health and safety?* The steel crisis which ran from mid-July until early November, 1959, is the latest of a long series of critical disputes. In twelve years it has been thought necessary to invoke the emergency disputes provisions of the Taft-Hartley Act on sixteen occasions. Since 1945 there have been five major steel strikes. Two nationwide railroad strikes were averted by drastic presidential intervention after the machinery of the Railway Labor Act had been exhausted. A more serious dispute looms over the horizon. East coast shipping has been tied up five times during the same period.

Of course there are opposing considerations which should temper the demand for new legislation. The country has survived each apparent crisis without a catastrophe. The costs of great strikes are wildly exaggerated because the press never balances the production, sales, and wages lost during a strike against the greater production and higher sales and wage payments during the preceding and succeeding periods. There is good reason to believe that many strikes are only a substitute for layoffs or shortened workweeks. Furthermore, when we measure the net loss of a strike, we are counting the price of greater economic freedom. Yet these are only tempering forces; they should not block the search for a solution.

2. *In basic industries can we continue to rely upon private negotiations between management and labor without government participation to establish wage levels and terms and conditions of employment? If not, what are the alternatives?* In raising this question I am less concerned with 1960 or 1961 than with the long-run trend of the national labor policy. The strain which the next quarter century will put upon the economy is reason enough for inquiring into conceivable adaptations.

For the most part I shall discuss these questions separately, but it is convenient to consider them together in examining the thesis that it is the excessive power of labor unions that endangers the public interest because it enables them not only to shut down essential industries, thereby endangering the public health and safety, but also to secure excessive wage increases, thereby accelerating the spiral of inflation. The remedy, some say, is to deprive labor unions of the immunity from the antitrust laws which they gained as a result of Supreme Court decisions under the Norris-LaGuardia Act.[3]

I

The Sherman Act was applied to labor unions from 1890 until about 1940 chiefly as a vehicle for the judicial formulation of labor policy upon the basis of the means and objectives tests. Injunctions were issued against strikes, boycotts, or picketing if the judge was satisfied that the union's objective did not justify the intentional infliction of harm to the employer's business. The size of the union, its bargaining power, and the effect of its activities upon the market were irrelevant. Even in the late 1930's, when the Department of Justice opened a brief campaign against alleged restraints of trade by labor unions, the courts were not concerned with the size of unions or monopolistic power but with practices held to be undesirable from the standpoint of labor relations, such as jurisdictional strikes and secondary boycotts. There is nothing in experience to indicate how the Sherman Act can be used effectively to prevent the growth of excessive union power or to avoid the conditions giving rise to emergency disputes.[4]

Indeed the basic theory and concepts of the antitrust laws are inapplicable to labor unions. The antitrust laws are designed to insure free markets by preserving and enforcing competition among a sufficient number of buyers and sellers of goods and services with sufficiently equal power to prevent anyone from controlling prices, supplies, or quality to the detriment of consumers. But labor unions do not compete against each other in the sale of labor. Can anyone imagine three or four unions of aircraft workers competing against each other for the privilege of supplying labor to Douglas, Lockheed, and North American? The only way in which competition can be restored among the sellers of labor is to destroy the labor unions so that individual workers will undersell each other, or at least to create a large enough pool of nonunion labor to be a threat to the bargaining power of unions.

---

[3] United States v. Hutcheson, 312 U.S. 219 (1940).

[4] For detailed discussions of the application of antitrust laws to labor unions, see Cox, *Labor and the Anti-Trust Laws—A Preliminary Analysis,* 104 U. PA. L. REV. 252 (1955); *Smith, Anti-Trust Laws and Labor,* 53 MICH. L. REV. 1119 (1955).

The Hartley bill and the Ball amendment of 1947 proposed to eliminate "industry-wide bargaining" (a misnomer for industry-wide unionization) by confining the bargaining rights of each union to a single employer, and then forbidding the several company-wide unions to combine or conspire by coordinating their negotiations either directly or through an international union. In the automobile industry there would be one union for Ford, one for General Motors, one for Chrysler, and one for each of the smaller companies. The same pattern would be enforced throughout the economy, with a possible exception for very small firms in a single industrial area, such as the garment shops in New York City.[5]

Obviously this proposal would provide no safeguard against national emergency disputes arising at a single plant. In 1952–1953 a strike at one plant of the American Locomotive Co. cut off the entire supply of a nickel alloy pipe used in the gaseous diffusion plants of the Atomic Energy Commission. In 1952 only the personal intervention of President Truman avoided a strike against North American Aviation, the only producer of jet airplanes needed in the Korean conflict.

In extreme cases it is possible to assert that one side of the bargaining table or the other has an excessive preponderance of bargaining power. The Wagner Act's reference to equalizing bargaining power[6] escaped being nonsense because the scales were then tipped heavily in favor of employers. Today there are small employers who lack the power to bargain effectively with the Teamsters or the United Automobile Workers, but it would seem easier to encourage them to increase their power by NLRA amendments encouraging multi-employer bargaining units than to attempt to weaken the powerful unions.[7] It seems impossible, however, to formulate a standard by which a disinterested observer can judge when a union has too much power in relation to the employers with whom it deals. One measures a labor union's power not by direct comparison with the number and size of other unions selling in the same market, as one does in the case of business firms, but in relation to the countervailing power of the employers with whom it deals. How can we determine whether the United Steelworkers is

[5] H.R. 3020, 80th Cong., 1st Sess. For later versions see H.R. 8449, 82d Cong., 2d Sess. (1952), by Mr. Gwinn and H.R. 2545, 83d Cong., 1st Sess. (1953), by Mr. Lucas.

[6] NLRA § 1.

[7] For example, the NLRB might be authorized to set up a multi-employer unit where there had been pattern bargaining even though there was no history of bargaining in such a unit. For the union to negotiate with one member of a multi-employer unit might be made an unfair labor practice.

more powerful than the United States Steel Corporation and whether the United Automobile Workers has greater bargaining power than General Motors?

Breaking up the international unions would hardly affect the course of negotiations in the oligopolistic industries such as those that produce steel, automobiles, and copper. One could hardly expect each company-wide union to negotiate without an eye upon the others; the companies do not make prices in that fashion. Recently the International Association of Machinists permitted the local unions which represented employees on each of several major airlines to conduct decentralized negotiations, company by company, making their own decisions upon wage policy. The result was a succession of strikes because each company-wide group sought to leap-frog to a higher wage over the preceding settlement. The aluminum, aircraft, and lumber industries, where there were rival unions for years, have felt the same wage pressures as if there were one.

In industries where the firms are smaller, breaking the labor movement into company-wide fragments, with each forbidden to bargain in consultation with another fragment or a parent international, would affect the course of collective bargaining by weakening some labor unions and destroying a great many. The employees of a single company are too small a unit to support the experienced officials and professional staff required to negotiate and administer contracts effectively. But these are not the industries in which the inflationary wage pressures are serious nor, except for coal mining, do they experience national emergency disputes. The great vice of the proposed antitrust weapon, therefore, is that it would kill and maim innocent bystanders, while leaving the ostensible targets unaffected.

Even if such a program were theoretically sound, it is impractical. A program of breaking up labor organizations could not succeed unless it was accompanied by vigorous efforts to break up giant corporations. They will not be broken up. We cannot turn back the clock despite our nostalgia for a simpler economy. Although labor unions impose some restraints upon competition with which the law might deal,[8] the antitrust laws provide no solution to national emergency disputes and no security for the public interest in the substantive terms of the settlements.

[8] See Cox, *supra* note 4.

II

In examining other solutions to the problem of national emergency disputes it is important to note the critical dilemma. The community desires both the elimination of strikes from vital industries *and* free collective bargaining. Unhappily, the community can never realize both wishes; strikes and collective bargaining are inseparable. The task of the legislator until the community makes a clear-cut choice, which is not the way of democracy, is to find the workable accommodation which will bring the largest measure of satisfaction in terms of both desiderata, though a bit of each must be sacrificed in order to attain enough of the other.

Even in management circles there is wide agreement upon the inadequacy of the emergency dispute provisions of the Taft-Hartley Act.[9] The Boards of Inquiry, which are charged with reporting the facts to the President before he seeks an injunction and again after sixty days, have sometimes engaged in useful mediation, but they can do no more. The injunction may forestall calamity by keeping the wheels of industry turning for an additional eighty days. It takes the leadership "off the hook" if management or union blunders into an unwanted strike, or if the rank-and-file employees compel union officials to sanction a strike against their better judgment. In the typical case, however, the injunction simply postpones the showdown at the price of relieving both employer and employees of the pressures which might have caused a settlement. In 1959 the steel companies would have felt the pressure to make concessions earlier if the likelihood that operations could be resumed under an injunction had not furnished an easier answer to the clamor of their customers and the fear for their ore supplies due to the onset of winter. Employees grow more obstinate when put back to work under a court decree. All the disputes handled under the Taft-Hartley procedure, except two, have been settled either at the outset or after the injunction was lifted and the renewal of the strike increased the pressure to compromise.[10]

It is sometimes said that the real pressure for a settlement under the Taft-Hartley Act comes from the balloting which the government conducts upon the employer's last offer of settlement, because a vote to accept the offer would put irresistible pressure upon the union leaders.

---

[9] LMRA §§ 206–210.

[10] The Taft-Hartley experience is reviewed in Rehmus, *Operation of the National Emergency Provisions of the LMRA*, 62 YALE L.J. 1047 (1953); EMERGENCY DISPUTES AND NATIONAL POLICY 91–146 (Bernstein et al. eds. 1955).

The steel strike might have provided conclusive proof, but the evidence available shows that the employees almost always support their leaders. Furthermore, the political strategy of the referendum distracts both sides, but especially the union leaders, from collective bargaining just when negotiations are most important. The future, if not the existence, of the union is at stake. The resulting emotionalism, especially if there is a big vote against the company's offer, may make it even harder for the union leaders to make necessary concessions.

As dissatisfaction with the Taft-Hartley solution spreads, so is there a growing body of opinion that the best hope for avoiding national emergency strikes, while preserving a large measure of freedom and private responsibility in the terms of the settlement, lies in legislation which opens the door to a wide choice of procedures. While this approach seems promising, in my judgment it should be combined with measures which impose upon each industry the primary responsibility for working out its own solution.

Standing Industry Procedures. Each industry in which a labor dispute might affect the national health or safety should be placed under a statutory admonition to create a standing procedure for resolving disputes which will not yield to the ordinary processes of negotiation. Among the possibilities are private mediation, fact-finding with or without recommendations, voluntary arbitration, or reference to a permanent bipartite industry board vested with power to decide by a stipulated majority. The essential points are (1) that it be a standing procedure which survives the termination of regular collective bargaining agreements; (2) that it come into play at an early stage in negotiations before positions have hardened; and (3) that it give *reasonable* assurance of avoiding an emergency. The Railway Labor Act already provides a standing procedure for the railroad and airline industries.

Recent history makes one somewhat pessimistic as to the likelihood that labor and management will shoulder this responsibility, but there are strong reasons for pursuing what hope there is until the end. Experience under the Railway Labor Act, despite recent failures, and in atomic energy installations seems to show that the best settlement procedures are those devised by management and labor for their own industry, taking into account its peculiar background, technology, customs, and needs. The primary responsibility would be put squarely upon the private parties, management and labor, who must realize that if they wish to preserve freedom to fix wages and conditions of employment by collective bargaining, they must demonstrate their willingness and ability to safeguard the public interest. It is no answer for each to point the finger at the other. The public is entitled to know when they have failed.

The establishment of standing procedures would also take account of the fact that the central issues in labor relations have become too complicated to resolve by splitting the last nickel or finding a happy formula under pressure of a crisis. Consider, for example, the complexities of increasing industrial productivity by electronic devices or atomic energy while making adequate provision for human costs and a just allocation of the monetary savings. The resolution of the work-rules issue on the railroads will require complete revision of an elaborate structure, including methods of wage payment, which dates back to 1920.

The government cannot compel an industry to take these steps, but it can apply pressure and offer assistance. The statute should provide that upon request of an industry or a finding by the Secretary of Labor that an industry has failed to establish an industry procedure, the President should appoint a Board of Public Responsibility chosen from men of experience and high standing in the field of industrial relations who would remain private citizens but would serve as the occasion required. Such a board should have two duties: (1) to assist the industry in setting up its own procedure; and (2) to serve the functions of an industry procedure whenever there was none. Except for this and the normal work of the Federal Mediation and Conciliation Service, the government should not be brought into the first stage of the procedure. The White House and cabinet officers cannot follow labor negotiations through all their stages. The participation of staff employees would accomplish nothing.

Presidential Intervention. Notwithstanding industry procedures, there will always be some critical disputes. The statute should therefore establish a National Emergency Disputes Board which the President would summon and consult whenever the Secretary of Labor certified the existence of an unresolved dispute which he had cause to believe was an imminent threat to the national health or safety. The Board should be composed of the Secretaries of Defense, Commerce, and Labor, and two eminent citizens, one with a background in management and the other from labor, but neither of them currently associated with parties to the controversy. Sidney Weinburg and Clinton Golden illustrate the type of men required. The National Emergency Disputes Board should have three functions:

1. The National Emergency Disputes Board should arrange a settlement, if possible, or a method of obtaining a settlement without the cessation of normal operations.

2. The Board should make all possible arrangements for protecting the national interest in the event of a strike or lockout. If we are serious in our desire to preserve free collective bargaining, of which a few strikes are an inescapable part, we should spend more effort upon finding makeshift arrangements, however drastic, for ensuring the supply of truly essential goods and services during a strike.

3. The Board should hear the parties and advise the President upon the single question whether a strike or lockout would do immediate harm to the national health or safety. The hearing would not only deter hasty government action, but also focus public pressure upon the parties.

If the President finds after studying the report of the Emergency Disputes Board that an emergency is imminent, he should have statutory authority to follow five courses of action, singly, consecutively, or concurrently:

1. He might appoint a fact-finding board with power to mediate and also to make public recommendations for the settlement of the dispute.

2. A Board of Inquiry might be appointed for the purpose of arranging voluntary arbitration, or, if this fails, reporting to the public the blame for imperiling the national health or safety rather than accepting an impartial decision. Fear of public indignation, properly focused, would probably lead to more acceptance of voluntary arbitration.

3. Since an injunction may be the only way to stop a strike, the statute should authorize the President to obtain an injunction for as long as he deems appropriate but not more than six months. The public health and safety are more important than the rights of either party.

4. The President should also have power to seize and operate the industrial property affected by the dispute. Such a step would be as distasteful to employers as injunctions are to unions, but the aim is to make presidential intervention objectionable to both. Since strikes would be forbidden during the period of government operation, the President should be authorized, but not required, to appoint a Wage Adjustment Board to recommend any changes in wages and conditions of employment for the period of government operation. The parties would be under heavy pressure to adopt these interim conditions as the terms of the final settlement in order to terminate the seizure, but the appearance of voluntarism and some of the reality would be preserved. The pressure is less than under compulsory arbitration, which I reject

even as an available procedure upon the ground that it would too easily become the normal course.

In Massachusetts the employer may elect either to allow the Commonwealth to operate the business for his financial account or else to sue for just compensation, the measure of which would presumably include an allowance for the employer's inability to use the strikebound property.[11] This method of financial adjustment seems to have worked pretty well, but I am inclined to think that the government should also have the right of electing to pay only just compensation; otherwise, seizure might become a sham—a method of breaking strikes without disturbing the management's control of the owner's profits.

The term "seizure" has a tyrannical sound. It is a drastic measure, but sometimes employers and unions are willing to settle their disputes only when confronted with dire alternatives. Nor is seizure a novel remedy. Its use by the federal government began in 1918. It was fairly common in World War II.[12] Several states have seizure statutes, notably Massachusetts and Missouri.[13] When a business becomes financially insolvent, an equity or bankruptcy court may assume possession and control, and operate the business for the benefit of interested persons. Seizure is little more than an executive receivership imposed because the company and union are insolvent in their labor relations.

5. Finally, the President should be given his most important power in explicit terms—the power to do nothing. Sometimes the parties negotiate agreements very promptly after they are convinced that no one else will carry the burden.

In academic discourse it is easy to argue that the country has never faced a true emergency as a result of a peacetime strike, that the President would have ample constitutional authority to deal with a crisis, and that we can best preserve collective bargaining by repealing all legislation applicable to emergency disputes. In my opinion muddling through will not meet the challenges of the atomic age and space exploration; but the debate is largely irrelevant because the public's answer will surely be that of

> ... the faith healer from Diehl
> Who said, "I know pain isn't real,
> But when I puncture my skin
> With the point of a pin
> I dislike what I fancy I feel."

[11] MASS. GEN. LAWS (Ter. Ed.) c. 150B, § 4.

[12] For a detailed discussion of seizure, see Teller, *Government Seizure in Labor Disputes*, 60 HARV. L. REV. 1017 (1947).

[13] MASS. GEN. LAWS (Ter. Ed.) c. 150B; MO. REV. STAT. § 10178.

The flexibility of the choice-of-procedure approach is an important asset, but the chief advantage over other remedies lies in its capacity for preserving uncertainty as to the form and extent of government intervention. Any set course of procedure enters into the parties' calculations, with the result that their negotiations tend to run the full course before they buckle down to business. This weakness has frequently developed under the Railway Labor and Taft-Hartley Acts; the 1950 coal strike is one illustration, the 1959 steel strike is another. In ordinary labor negotiations the risks and costs of a strike are among the most powerful factors in bringing about an agreement. Since these forces are largely inoperative when the cessation of operations would endanger the public, the choice-of-procedures approach substitutes new uncertainties. Some alternatives would be objectionable to employers, others to unions. The stage would be set for active mediation, going far beyond exhortations and expressions of good will, in which the President neither hesitated to influence the substance of the bargaining nor allowed the parties to forget that the choice of his procedure, in the event of continued disagreement, might be influenced by his judgment as to who was to blame for the want of a settlement. Thus armed with a variety of weapons, the Chief Executive would probably be spared the use of any.

The policy of the Eisenhower Administration, until the final settlement of the 1959 steel dispute, has been to avoid government interference with collective bargaining. One might object to my suggestions upon the ground that the previous policy was correct or else go to the other extreme and argue that the suggestions invite so much government participation that it would be better to formalize the government's responsibility by establishing a labor court or wage regulation board. Neither position can be adequately considered without facing the still more fundamental questions whether the next quarter century should bring changes in the American system of industrial relations which will increase the government's participation in establishing wage levels and other conditions of employment; and if so, what form should the participation take.

III

During the next twenty-five years the strain which the military budget has already put upon the economy will continue to increase. Upheavals in Africa, Asia, and, one fears, South America, though they mark enormous material progress, make it unlikely that international tensions will relax, whatever our relations with the Soviet Union. The irresistible challenge of space exploration will exhaust great treasure. The exploding population will produce, but it will also require large increases in the production of goods and vast outlays for schools, highways, and public services. The capacity of the economy will be greatly enlarged by automation and later by the use of atomic energy, but the revolutionary character of these changes will itself strain human institutions.

Another moment's reflection is enough to demonstrate the public importance of the bargains struck between management and labor in basic industries. The current steel dispute affords two obvious examples: wages and work rules.

Although the economists closely associated with management exaggerate the inflationary tendency of collective bargaining while those close to labor argue that large wage increases are the best corrective, most independent scholars seem to agree that the continual increases in wages and fringe betterments contributed significantly to inflation because they pushed costs up to the point where further wage increases were requisite.[14] The effect spreads from a basic industry not only because the material enters into other products but also because the precedent affects other labor negotiations. The short-run interests of management and labor in a wage negotiation may be opposed to the public interest. Employees are naturally anxious to improve their economic position relative to the rest of the community. Firms that do not have to worry about price competition, either because of the nature of the industry or because their competitors face the same union demands, may find it more profitable to avoid a strike by raising both wages and prices. One does not have to argue that inflation is always an evil to maintain that the public has an interest in the question. The government controls or influences many other factors that affect the growth of the economy and the value of money—expenditures, tax policy, interest rates, and credit. Wage levels are debated by the negotiators in basic industries largely in terms of broad policies which will affect the entire nation. It seems more than a little curious, therefore, that those charged with advancing the interests of special groups should be the only participants in the decision. The very same question would arise, of course, whenever the danger was deflation.

[14] Duesenberry, *Underlying Factors in the Post-War Inflation,* in WAGES, PRICES, PROFITS AND PRODUCTIVITY (Proceedings of Fifteenth American Assembly 1959) 61–89; Slichter, *Labor Costs and Prices,* in WAGES, PRICES, PROFITS AND PRODUCTIVITY (Proceedings of Fifteenth American Assembly 1959) 167–180; *Hearings before the Joint Committee upon the Economic Report of the President,* 86th Cong., 1st Sess. (1959) (testimony of John T. Dunlop).

The work-rules issue in the 1959 steel dispute is also a useful example because there is less danger that the short-run interests of management and labor will coincide to the detriment of the public. One aspect of the question related to thousands of specific operations but at bottom it was, how can industry make the most effective utilization of labor with due regard to human values? The other aspect was, how shall this decision be made—by management alone or by management and the union jointly? Although only the latter issue appeared to be at stake in the negotiations, the two questions are obviously interrelated. Under ordinary conditions there could be little doubt about the desirability of leaving the problem to collective bargaining to be solved in various ways in various businesses at different times and different places, but the adaptation of electronic devices to a wide variety of industrial uses makes the questions not only more acute but more pervasive. It is no longer the process of periodic technological change which confronts us, affecting first one job and then another, but a revolution potentially involving the displacement of 20 or 25 per cent of the work force of entire industries. The pace of the transition, the retraining or other protection of displaced workers, the participation of union representatives to give employees assurance that their interests are protected, all have obvious public importance. The opposition of the selfish interests of management and labor gives fairly good assurance that no radical mistakes will be made in reaching decisions, though the slow pace of technological change in some aspects of the construction industry makes one wonder; but this is no guarantee that they will be right in every instance. Even if they are, active public participation may be required to carry out the best solution.

If the argument up to this point seems to be a vague, theoretical plea for a greater degree of planning, let me hasten to emphasize the objections to detailed government determination of wages or other conditions of employment. Distrust of the cumbersome apparatus necessary for detailed control of the economy was one of the chief lessons learned by those who participated in the administration of wage and price controls during World War II and the Korean incident. Perhaps the worst feature is the rigidity of regulation even in the hands of imaginative and skilled administrators, rigidity in applying rules to remote situations whose variations and subtleties defy explanation at a distance and also rigidity in changing rules out of tune with events. But this objection and others such as the mediocrity of a permanent bureaucracy carry force only so long as one is speaking of widespread controls at all levels of the economy. The collective bargaining negotiations which raise important public issues are the pace-setters—the negotiations in basic industries which, because of psychological or economic forces, affect the entire economy. If the public interest were to make itself felt at this point, there would be no need for a bureaucracy, and flexibility and individual initiative could be preserved through thousands of ensuing private decisions.

Our dedication to free collective bargaining, as I remarked at the outset, also rests upon a moral philosophy. Private decision-making increases personal opportunity and responsibility. Reliance upon government lessens man's power of choice between good and evil; it makes him less a man. In a complex society of organized groups the individual's power to influence events is limited, his participation in decisions is vicarious, but so long as private decision-making prevails, a pluralistic society preserves power of choice and therefore the responsibility for the decision. But I wonder whether greater governmental participation would not preserve, or indeed increase, pluralism and opportunities for vicarious participation in the decision-making process in basic wage negotiations. Is it realistic to describe bargains struck between the president of the United Steelworkers and the chairman of the board of U. S. Steel Corpóration as a democratic process in which those affected by a decision have the responsibility for making it? It is more democratic than if either made the decision alone, but the addition of a third chair at the bargaining table would further diffuse authority and further increase the vicarious participation of those affected. The general public is vitally affected, but currently its spokesman, the government, has not even the right to a hearing.

I use the phrase "addition of a third chair at the bargaining table" because the crux of the matter is the form of government participation. The vice in government determination is that it carries the force of law. Compulsion is efficient in theory, but by making the job too easy it reduces the challenge to creative imagination. We progress not by giving orders but by finding new accommodations. William H. Davis, the wise philosopher of collective bargaining, expressed the thought so effectively in a recent article that I would like to quote a passage, even though his friends may allude to the devil's quoting scripture for his own purpose.

> The establishment of conditions of employment by agreement . . . is the manifestation in industrialized societies of the pregnant fact that in the life of mankind creation is the victory of persuasion over force. . . .

> ... [C]ompulsion can have a benign effect insofar as it establishes behavior essential to social welfare, yet it is always accompanied by the baneful effect that it stops the *progress* of civilization....
>
> ... We grow in character and dignity not by compulsion in our relations with one another, but by reasoned agreement. The knowledge of good and evil and the freedom to choose the better and reject the worse, with which we are uniquely endowed, here comes into play.... It is upon them that we rely for the liberty of thought and action through which we visualize the upward adventure of life on earth.[15]

But compulsion is not an inescapable ingredient of governmental participation. The tripartite War Labor Board rested upon a basic consensus of public, labor, and management opinion formed under pressure of emergency; the participation of labor and management was not wholly voluntary but neither was it coerced by law. The Wage Stabilization Board of the Korean period strove to find, and sometimes temporarily achieved, a foundation in common consent. The government's need to win consent is demonstrated by the collapse of wage and price controls in 1952 before the power of the U. S. Steel Corporation and later under pressure from the United Mine Workers of America.

It is unlikely that the exact tripartite arrangement of the wartime and Korean periods will be promptly restored, perhaps not ever. In the immediate future less drastic forms of government participation must be devised. The most practicable starting point may be the regular annual or biennial conferences of senior government, labor, and management officials, suggested by Professor Dunlop,[16] for discussion of the public consequences of the decisions to be made in ensuing contract negotiations. The discussion should go far beyond general exhortation into detailed facts and figures. Although not a negotiation session and not aimed at formal agreements, there should be a genuine interchange of views upon the key issues.

Such a conference is only a first step. The forms through which government influence might be brought to bear more directly and with greater force remain to be devised, as do the techniques for ensuring that private decision-making in other segments of the economy would not undercut the policies followed in basic industries under governmental pressure. But we should welcome the fact-finding boards with power to make recommendations, Boards of Inquiry, and other special commissions mentioned in the discussion of national emergency disputes, as opportunities to add to our store of substantive concepts and methods of tripartite participation.

---

[15] Davis, *Should Labor Be Coerced?* 189 NATION 372 (1959).

[16] Dunlop, *loc. cit. supra* note 14.

One last, still vague thought requires expression. The rents in the fabric of society, which are growing frighteningly wide and deep because of conflicts in industrial relations, can be mended only by a renewal of faith in the powers of reason. Over one hundred years ago George Bancroft wrote: "The feud between the capitalist and laborer, the House of Have and the House of Want, is as old as social union and can never be entirely quieted; but he who will act with moderation, prefer fact to theory, and remember that everything in this world is relative and not absolute, will see that the violence of the contest may be stilled."[17]

[17] Bancroft, Letter to the Workingmen of Northampton, Boston Courier, Oct. 22, 1834.

Chapter 4

The Role of Law in the Administration of Labor Agreements

One reflecting upon the role of law in the administration of collective bargaining agreements can hardly avoid beginning with the thought that the institutions of collective bargaining evolved and flourished outside of the courts and often in the face of legal interference. By the 1930's law had fallen into disrepute in the world of labor-management relations, because it failed to meet the needs of men. Although legal scholars spun interesting theories,[1] the blunt truth was that collective bargaining agreements were negotiated without much regard to conventional legal sanctions.

At first most disputes arising under existing agreements were settled by direct negotiations or strikes, but as labor agreements grew in complexity and began to cover wider segments of industrial life, it became obvious that strikes were too costly a method of resolving disputes in the day-to-day administration of a collective bargaining agreement. In the 1940's the trend toward arbitration by a third party was accelerated by the wartime necessity for peaceful methods of settlement.[2] Management and labor, aided by neutral experts, were extraordinarily creative in constructing forums and procedures. Some have retained the simple device of calling in an *ad hoc* arbitrator to determine the dispute.[3] Other industries have established standing tribunals with a permanent umpire at the apex of an elaborate structure.[4] Today 90 or 95 per cent

[1] *E.g.*, Rice, *Collective Labor Agreements in American Law*, 44 HARV. L. REV. 572 (1931).

[2] The impact of War Labor Board policies is best described in Freidin and Ulman, *Arbitration and the National War Labor Board*, 58 HARV. L. REV. 309 (1945).

[3] The purely administrative features of *ad hoc* arbitration can be given a degree of stability by a stipulation calling for arbitration under the rules of the American Arbitration Association.

[4] For a discussion of two such systems, see Wolff et al., *The Chrysler–UAW Umpire System*, in PROCEEDINGS OF THE ELEVENTH ANNUAL MEETING OF THE NATIONAL ACADEMY OF ARBITRATORS 111–148 (1958); Alexander, *The General Motors–UAW Experience*, in PROCEEDINGS OF THE TWELFTH ANNUAL MEETING OF THE NATIONAL ACADEMY OF ARBITRATORS 108–160 (1959).

of the employees covered by collective agreements work in establishments where there is grievance arbitration.[5]

Each autonomous, private legal system tended to create by custom and convention, as well as by arbitration, the "rights," "duties," and "relationships" necessary to govern men's industrial lives within the basic framework of the collective bargaining agreement. The system worked so well on the whole that Harry Shulman, perhaps the most perceptive of arbitrators, argued that even when the autonomous system established by the parties broke down, the law should stand aside for fear of injuring other going systems.[6]

Today, for better or worse, we are set upon a different course. Congress made the decisive turn in 1947, when it provided in Section 301 of the Labor Management Relations Act that "Suits for violation of contracts between an employer and a labor organization representing employeees in an industry affecting commerce . . . may be brought in any district court of the United States. . . ."[7] The statute itself obviously established the principle that a collective agreement is a legally enforceable contract. It provides a forum in which labor organizations may sue or be sued as legal entities, an important departure from the common-law rule which treats them as collections of individual men and women, each of whom would have to be named a party to the litigation. Ten years later, in *Textile Workers Union v. Lincoln Mills of Alabama*,[8] the Supreme Court enunciated two additional rules:

1. Section 301 creates a body of federal law governing rights and remedies under collective bargaining agreements in industries affecting interstate commerce.

2. One of the rules in this body of federal law is that the courts will enforce the arbitration clause of a collective bargaining agreement.

[5] Howard, *Labor-Management Arbitration*, 21 Mo. L. Rev. 1, 4 (1956).

[6] Shortly before his death Dean Shulman gave us a notable statement of this view that the law should stay out of grievance arbitration: "[Arbitration] is a means of making collective bargaining work and thus preserving private enterprise in a free government. When it works fairly well, it does not need the sanction of the law of contracts or the law of arbitration. It is only when the system breaks down completely that the courts' aid in these respects is invoked. But the courts cannot, by occasional sporadic decision, restore the parties' continuing relationship; and their intervention in such cases may seriously affect the going systems of self-government. When their autonomous system breaks down, might not the parties better be left to the usual methods for adjustment of labor disputes rather than to court actions on the contract or on the arbitration award? I suggest that the law stay out—but, mind you, not the lawyers." Shulman, *Reason, Contract, and Law in Labor Relations*, 68 Harv. L. Rev. 999, 1024 (1955).

[7] 61 Stat. 156 (1947), 29 U.S.C. § 185 (1952).

[8] 353 U.S. 448 (1957).

The *Lincoln Mills* decision creates whole congeries of legal problems, but there appear to be two central issues corresponding, but in reverse order, to the principles established by the decision:

1. How can grievance arbitration be fitted into the surrounding legal structure without destroying its value as a system of industrial self-government? The legal slate is never quite clean, but the federal courts are now in a position to write a law of grievance arbitration substantially free from precedent.

2. What is the legal nature of a collective bargaining agreement? It is in the most fictitious sense that Section 301 creates a body of federal law governing rights under a labor contract. In simpler words, it authorizes the court to create one. Wise rules of law cannot be established without conscious reflection upon the nature of the institutions they are to govern, even though under the common-law practice the theory grows with the decisions.

In the end both questions have a common core. Fitting arbitration into the legal system also requires an understanding of its nature, which in turn results from the nature of the agreement which the arbitrator is helping to administer. The perception and skill with which the questions are answered will determine whether the entry of law into the administration of labor contracts is a bane or a blessing. The gap which enabled grievance arbitration to grow up free from legal obstacles has now become dangerous; for the arbitrators and many labor lawyers are overly immersed in their own special milieu, while the judges who are suddenly projected into the area lack knowledge of the special ways of collective bargaining and therefore tend to deal with a labor contract as they would a bill of sale, a lease, a deed, or a trust indenture. The judges' disapproval of the views of arbitrators is exceeded only by the arbitrators' dismay at judicial decisions.[9]

[9] For formal criticisms of the court decisions see Summers, *Judicial Review of Labor Arbitration*, 2 BUFFALO L. REV. 1 (1952); Scoles, *Review of Labor Arbitration Awards on Jurisdictional Grounds*, 17 U. CHI. L. REV. 606 (1950). The attitude of arbitrators is constantly reflected in the Proceedings of the National Academy of Arbitrators. See, *e.g., Critical Issues in Labor Arbitration*, in PROCEEDINGS OF THE TENTH ANNUAL MEETING OF THE NATIONAL ACADEMY OF ARBITRATORS 112–143 (1957); *Arbitration and the Law*, in PROCEEDINGS OF THE TWELFTH ANNUAL MEETING OF THE NATIONAL ACADEMY OF ARBITRATORS 1–89 (1959).

I

The bridge between grievance arbitration and the law is the suit to compel performance of an agreement to arbitrate or to enforce, or set aside, an arbitration award.[10] In such litigation the critical issues revolve about the slippery concept of "arbitrability." Our footing will be more secure if we start with the self-evident premise that Section 301 covers only "Suits for violation of contracts," which means suits to enforce a promise or to recover damages for its breach. In a proceeding to compel arbitration the promise is the undertaking to submit a universal or limited class of disputes to an arbitrator, and then to carry out his award. The plaintiff must lose unless he shows that the defendant violated the promise. Obviously the court must decide whether the plaintiff has made his case. It follows that the court must decide whether the dispute which the plaintiff wishes to arbitrate is a dispute of the kind which the defendant promised to arbitrate. Using the term "arbitrable" to denote any issue covered by the arbitration agreement, it is accurate to say that the plaintiff can never prevail unless he shows the existence of an arbitrable question; and in this sense it is fair to say that the question of arbitrability is always for the court, as indeed the courts uniformly rule.[11]

In another sense the statement is inaccurate. An employer and the union representing his employees may agree to the standard clause calling for arbitration of "any dispute as to the interpretation or application of any provision of this agreement," but they might also add a further undertaking to arbitrate any dispute concerning the scope of the arbitration clause. Suppose now that the union complained that the company had violated the contract by subcontracting production work to other manufacturers; that the company refused to arbitrate upon the ground that the contract did not mention the subject of subcontracting; and that the union replied that the restriction inhered in the very nature of the collective agreement. If the union sued to compel arbitration, one question of arbitrability would be for the court, i.e., whether defendant had broken a promise to arbitrate; and on this point the union would

[10] This problem and others covered by this lecture are discussed in more detail in my earlier article, *Reflections upon Labor Arbitration*, 72 HARV. L. REV. 1482 (1959) The lecture draws heavily upon the article even to the point of incorporating some paragraphs without revision.

[11] See Local 149, Am. Fed'n of Technical Engineers v. General Electric Co., 250 F.2d 922, 927 (1st Cir. 1957), *cert. denied*, 356 U.S. 938 (1958); American Lava Corp. v. Local 222, UAW, 250 F.2d 137 (6th Cir. 1958) (per curiam).

prevail because the meaning of the arbitration clause is obviously arbitrable under the supposed contract. Another question of arbitrability would be for the arbitrator, i.e., whether the dispute over subcontracting was a question of "interpretation or application" within the power of the arbitrator to determine, for by hypothesis the parties promised to submit this question for his decision and this promise is as enforceable as the other.[12]

Unfortunately the conventional clause calling for arbitration of "any dispute concerning the interpretation or application of any provision of this agreement" is silent about the treatment of disputes concerning the meaning of the arbitration clause. One can argue with force that a dispute about the scope of the arbitration clause is a dispute about the meaning of a provision of the agreement. There is nothing startling in this distribution of power. Courts determine their own jurisdiction.[13] One wishing to challenge the jurisdiction of an administrative agency must raise the question before the agency and exhaust his administrative remedies upon the jurisdictional question as well as upon the merits before he may raise it in court, unless the agency action is a patent usurpation of power which would cause irreparable hardship.[14] The principal purpose of an arbitration clause—to provide a specialized tribunal for the relatively informal development of the facts—would be implemented by reading the contract as a delegation of power to decide what disputes fall within its scope. Allowing the arbitrator to interpret the arbitration clause would also economize time and effort. The evidence bearing upon questions of arbitrability is often relevant to the merits. The true nature of the claim may not be discernible until all the facts are in evidence. An appraisal of its character demands the same specialized experience with industrial relations as a decision on the merits.

Nevertheless, I am persuaded that the conventional arbitration clause does not allow an arbitrator to make a final determination of his own jurisdiction. The contrast between the conventional phraseology and a wide-open clause calling for arbitration of all disputes is too plain to put down to inadvertence. The narrower clause appears to be used because one party, usually the employer, distrusts arbitration at least

[12] In the Matter of Kelley, 240 N.Y. 74, 147 N.E. 363 (1925); Local 205, United Elec., Radio & Mach. Workers v. General Electric Co., 233 F.2d 85, 101 (1st Cir. 1956) (dictum), *aff'd*, 353 U.S. 547 (1957). But cf. Lodge 12, Int'l Ass'n of Machinists v. Cameron Iron Works, 257 F.2d 467 (5th Cir. 1958).

[13] United States v. United Mine Workers, 330 U.S. 258 (1947).

[14] Myers v. Bethlehem Shipbuilding Corp., 303 U.S. 41 (1938); 3 DAVIS, ADMINISTRATIVE LAW §§ 20.02, 20.09 (2d ed. 1958).

to the point of insisting upon the inclusion of some safeguard against the arbitrator's imposing upon him significant obligations not contemplated by the agreement. The clause does not tell what the arbitrator should not do. It tells what he cannot do. The protection sought by the employer would be drastically reduced by a construction which gave the arbitrator unlimited power to determine his own jurisdiction and merely warned against improper exercise, for as a practical matter he would then have the power to impose obligations outside the contract limited only by his own understanding. We can give effect to the underlying purpose only by excepting the interpretation of the arbitration clause from the general power to interpret, thus giving the court the duty to determine whether the claim which one side wishes to arbitrate gives rise to a dispute concerning the "interpretation and application" of the collective bargaining agreement. The court decisions sustain this position.[15]

The acceptance of this conclusion need not carry agreement with all the judicial rulings made in the name of arbitrability. Interpreting a promise to arbitrate disputes over the meaning of a contract as if it covered only questions upon which reasonable men could differ[16] is an obvious interference with the arbitrator's jurisdiction over the merits of the controversy. The same courts would give short shrift to any labor union which called a strike instead of submitting a grievance to arbitration and then sought to justify its position upon the ground that the union was so plainly right that the grievance was not arbitrable. Surely any issue as to the satisfaction of conditions precedent to arbitration is also arbitrable under the conventional clause, as the Supreme Court of New Hampshire decided despite a contrary ruling in the First Circuit.[17] And I shall show a little later that an arbitrator should be held to have power to sustain some grievances, again contrary to the view of the lower federal courts, even though there is no specific language in the contract upon which the claim can be founded.[18]

[15] In addition to the cases cited in note 11, see Local 201, Int'l Union of Electrical Workers v. General Electric Co., 262 F.2d 265 (1st Cir. 1959); Engineers Ass'n v. Sperry Rand Corp., 251 F.2d 133 (2d Cir. 1957).

[16] International Ass'n of Machinists v. Cutler-Hammer, Inc., 271 App. Div. 917, 67 N.Y.S.2d 317, *aff'd,* 297 N.Y. 519, 74 N.E.2d 464 (1947). *Contra,* New Bedford Defense Prods. Div. of Firestone Co. v. Local 1113, UAW, 258 F.2d 522 (1st Cir. 1958).

[17] Southwestern New Hampshire Transp. Co. v. Durham, 152 A.2d 596 (N.H. 1959). *Contra,* Boston Mutual Life Ins. Co. v. Ins. Agents' Int'l Union, 161 F. Supp. 222 (D. Mass. 1958).

[18] Local 149, Am. Fed'n of Technical Engineers v. General Electric Co., 250 F.2d 922, 924 (1st Cir. 1957), *cert. denied,* 356 U.S. 938 (1958).

II

One school of critics believes that the vitality of arbitration can be preserved from excessive judicial intervention only by legislation depriving the courts of power to rule upon questions of arbitrability. The arbitrator would first decide whether the dispute was of a character which the parties had agreed to submit to him for a final and binding decision and then, if his first answer was affirmative, he would decide the merits. The role of the court would be limited to determining whether the parties had a binding contract containing an arbitration clause of any character.

This division of functions seems entirely sound, both for the reasons mentioned above and because of the apparent failure of the courts to understand the ways of industrial arbitration. Nevertheless, I heartily oppose such legislation upon the ground that it would destroy the voluntary character of grievance arbitration. The point is easily illustrated by an example. Suppose that the only arbitration clause in a labor contract provides: "In the event that the parties are unable to adjust a grievance relating to seniority, discharge, or promotion, the grievance shall be submitted at the request of either party to final and binding arbitration under the rules of the American Arbitration Association." If the union brings suit to compel the employer to arbitrate a claim that the recognition clause of the contract bars subcontracting which would result in reduction of opportunities to work overtime, a decree compelling the employer to present his case to the arbitrator would rest upon statutory compulsion without an adequate foundation in consent, for obviously there was no agreement to submit this kind of dispute to arbitration. Furthermore, the legislation would reduce the number of agreements to arbitrate. Put to a choice between omitting an arbitration clause and accepting an arbitrator's decision upon all questions of arbitrability, many employers would refuse to arbitrate.

I do not mean to imply that nothing can be done by legislation to improve the relationship between arbitration and the courts. A number of doctrines criticized above should be overruled by statute. It would clarify some of the current uncertainty to prescribe the correct procedure, both in the trial court and upon appeal, and to specify the grounds upon which a court might set aside an arbitration award. Furthermore, the central difficulty today, as I shall show in a moment, is that most labor contracts fail to express an unequivocal intention as to whether the court or the arbitrator should rule on questions of arbitrability, because the parties either overlook the problem or cannot reach agreement upon the answer. The voluntary character of arbitration would not be impaired if a statute filled the ambiguous gap by creating a presumption that the issue of arbitrability was for the arbitrator in the first instance, unless a contrary intention was shown.

III

The best method of relating private methods of contract administration to the surrounding legal system is the more careful drafting of collective bargaining agreements.[19] Since judicial intervention rests upon the theory that the court is compelling performance of a promise, the parties may write their own prescription. For example, the parties might add to the conventional arbitration clause a sentence reading: "The arbitrator shall also have power to render a final and binding decision upon all questions concerning his jurisdiction or power, including questions concerning the scope, meaning, or application of the arbitration clause." If either the company or the union sought to litigate a question of arbitrability in court under this agreement, it would violate its promise and the plaintiff would secure an order for arbitration.[20] The only function of the court under such a contract would be the provision of legal sanctions for the agreement and resulting award.

If the suggested clause were thought too broad because it permits no check upon the arbitrator, the contract might provide:

> In the event that either party denies arbitrability of a dispute, the issue shall be submitted to the arbitrator. If he rules that the dispute is arbitrable, the case shall be heard by the arbitrator and a decision shall be rendered on the merits: *Provided*, that in any action which is brought to enforce or vacate the award the court shall have power to determine whether the dispute was arbitrable or the arbitrator otherwise exceeded his power.

This clause would give the employer the safeguard of an ultimate judicial ruling but it avoids the costs, delays, resentments, and dangers of judicial intervention prior to arbitration.

The possibilities for creative solutions are endless. General Electric Co. currently insists upon a clause calling for judicial rulings upon all questions of arbitrability before the arbitrator may proceed.[21] Those who prefer the other extreme can preserve complete autonomy by stipulating that the remedies provided by the contract shall be exclusive and that neither party will resort to any court or other tribunal.

---

[19] See Aaron, *On First Looking into the Lincoln Mills Decision*, in PROCEEDINGS OF THE TWELFTH ANNUAL MEETING OF THE NATIONAL ACADEMY OF ARBITRATORS 1 (1959).

[20] In addition to the authorities cited in note 12, see Freydberg Bros. v. Corey, 177 Misc. 560, 31 N.Y.S.2d 10 (Sup. Ct. 1941); Rogers Diesel & Aircraft Corp. v. Local 259, UAW, 15 L.R.R.M. 848 (N.Y. Sup. Ct. 1945).

[21] Aaron, *supra* note 19, at 9–10.

The contractual allocation of responsibility for deciding the scope of arbitration clauses will be a major factor in determining how far management and labor can continue to shape their own semi-autonomous jurisprudence to meet the peculiar needs of each bargaining unit. The conventional arbitration clause is given widely different meanings in different industries and at different plants. The subtle variations may have great importance to the parties. They can continue to control the growth of their relationship if they vest the arbitrator with power to determine the scope of his own jurisdiction, for not only do they choose the arbitrator but also he deems it a primary duty to reflect their interests and wishes. In the long run the preservation of this autonomy would seem more important to both management and labor than the protection afforded by reserving the right to a judicial decision upon the scope of the arbitrator's power.

IV

It would be naive, however, to suppose that any system of arbitration can indefinitely avoid the influence of judicial decisions. Legal analysis will influence arbitration by the force of competition and the interchange of ideas. Judges will find one method or another to avoid enforcing arbitration awards which they regard as unconscionable. Experienced bargainers will not ignore settled legal doctrines. Many employers will insist upon judicial rulings upon the power of the arbitrator. In the long run, the willingness to arbitrate, or to follow a particular form of arbitration, may be affected by any sharp divergence between the attitudes of arbitrators and the doctrines prevailing in judicial forums.

The legal profession should also be concerned about the flow of ideas to the federal courts. The Supreme Court has instructed the courts to fashion a law of collective bargaining agreements from the express provisions, the penumbra, and the policy of our national labor laws. "The range of judicial inventiveness will be determined by the nature of the problem."[22] The slate is relatively clean. Outside the area controlled by statute there is no more important treasury of experience than the record of grievance arbitrations. Surely arbitrators have not labored at the administration of collective agreements for almost two decades without arriving at some generalizations upon which the unbiased can agree, even though partisan interests preclude unanimity. Perhaps only a few rules have developed, but there are attitudes, approaches, and even a number of flexible principles. More effort may

[22]Textile Workers Union v. Lincoln Mills, 353 U.S. 448, 457 (1957).

have to go into distilling generalizations from the amorphous mass of arbitration opinions before the courts can be expected to use them. Counsel will face the further problem of translating the ways of the industrial world into legal doctrines comprehensible to judges who lack industrial experience. However, if the professional arbitrators and the labor lawyers who work with them can surmount these obstacles, the industrial jurisprudence which they have been developing might give wisdom and vitality to conventional law.

The core of the problem—the source of current divergence and the key to mutual support—lies in the development of a better understanding of the process of "interpretation and application" of a collective bargaining agreement. Even though the phrase is given different shades of meaning in different industries, everywhere in the industrial world it means more than ascertaining the dictionary meaning, or even the industrial meaning, of the words. Within the confines of the contract the arbitrator assists in building an industrial jurisprudence for the bargaining unit, often without much help from the words of the agreement. This point is so important that I wish to develop it at some length, first by concrete illustrations and then by discussing the peculiarities of the labor agreement which determine the nature of contract administration including the arbitration process. However, an initial word of caution seems appropriate. The parties are the arbitrator's masters. Any rule which they write into the contract, he must follow. He must guide himself by their conception of the arbitrator's function. A few contracts obviously reject the conception here described; others negate substantial portions; along the periphery every contract is unique. Only with these exceptions can one accurately say that the essential core of the arbitration process is determined by institutional characteristics of collective bargaining agreements, since they are pretty much the same in most industries; it takes rather plain language to justify any departure from the norm.

There are at least five areas in which arbitrators regularly base awards upon some foundation other than the language of the contract even though their jurisdiction is expressly limited to the adjudication of "disputes concerning the interpretation or application of any provision of this agreement."

1. Meaning must be poured into general phrases by the evaluation of a complex of interests and the development of subordinate rules. One cannot ascertain from the words whether working for a competitor[23]

[23] See, *e.g.*, Mechanical Handling Sys., Inc., 26 Lab. Arb. 401 (1956); Armen Berry Casing Co., 17 Lab. Arb. 179 (1950).

or being a Communist[24] is "just cause" for a discharge. A contract which stipulates that "promotions to higher paid jobs or better jobs with equal pay are based primarily upon merit and ability, but when these are equal the employee having the greatest seniority will receive preference" must be implemented by the development of subordinate rules governing such questions as what group shall be considered in making a promotion.[25] The arbitrator must lay down the rules if the parties have not agreed upon them. The contract is the ultimate source of the rights but it does not provide the actual criteria of decision.

2. Arbitrators frequently fashion remedies for breach of a collective agreement without a shred of contract language to guide them. If a contract forbidding discharge of employees without just cause is violated, an arbitrator will order reinstatement with or without back pay.[26] In a case at International Harvester Co., W. Willard Wirtz asserted authority to formulate a measure of damages when the employer violated the contract by failing to tell employees the piece rates at the start of a shift when they were transferred to temporary jobs.[27] At least two arbitration boards have imposed monetary penalties upon employees for breach of a no-strike clause.[28] The implication of power to afford a remedy rests upon the dictates of necessity. The power is essential to the successful functioning of the institution. Not a word in the average labor contract expresses the intention.

3. Grievance arbitration often involves the application of substantive doctrines which are not mentioned in the collective agreement. Suppose that a contract fixes a seven-day limit upon the appeal of grievances from the foreman's ruling and that the employee and shop steward wait ten days to appeal in reliance upon the personnel director's specific assurance that the company will not invoke the time limit. Surely there are only a few stern literalists who would deny the grievance without examining the merits if the company's attorney subsequently invoked the time limit. The customary disposition would be to ignore the time

---

[24] *Compare* Bethlehem Steel Co., 24 Lab. Arb. 852 (1955), *with* Pratt & Whitney Co., 28 Lab. Arb. 668 (1957).

[25] *E.g.*, Ford Motor Co., Opinion A-198, 1 P-H Lab. Arb. Awards 67604 (1945).

[26] Niles-Bement-Pond Co. v. Local 405, UAW, 140 Conn. 32, 97 A.2d 898 (1952); Samuel Adler, Inc. v. Local 584, Int'l Bhd. of Teamsters, 282 App. Div. 142, 122 N.Y.S.2d 8 (1953). *But see* Refinery Employees v. Continental Oil Co., 160 F. Supp. 723 (W.D. La. 1958), *aff'd*, 268 F.2d 447 (5th Cir. 1959), *cert. denied*, 361 U.S. 896 (1959).

[27] International Harvester Co., 9 Lab. Arb. 894 (1947).

[28] Newark Newsdealers Supply Co., 20 Lab. Arb. 476 (1953); Canadian Gen. Elec. Co., 18 Lab. Arb. 925 (1952).

limit upon grounds of waiver or estoppel.[29] The doctrine is based upon notions of justice. It has no foundation in the words of the contract.[30]

4. Collective bargaining agreements, like many commercial contracts, impose enforceable obligations which are not expressed in words. Suppose that during the term of a collective bargaining agreement an employer carried on a vigorous campaign of unfair labor practices designed to oust the incumbent bargaining representative, climaxing the campaign with the discharge of union officials. It is an ancient principle that "where a party stipulates that another shall do a certain thing, he thereby impliedly promises that he will himself do nothing which will hinder or obstruct the other in doing that thing."[31] Surely a gross attack upon the existence of a labor union increases the difficulty of its performing its contract obligations.[32]

Williston tells us that every contract contains "an implied covenant that neither party shall do anything which will have the effect of destroying or injuring the right of the other party to receive the fruits of the contract; in other words, in every contract there exists an implied covenant of good faith and fair dealing."[33] Suppose that a collective bargaining agreement contains seniority, grievance, and arbitration clauses, but that there are no words limiting the employer's freedom to discharge employees with or without just cause. During a seasonal decline in business which necessitates reduction in the working forces, the employer discharges the two senior employees in a fifteen-man department upon the ground that they are becoming bald, and retains the junior men. The union, showing that there is work for only thirteen men, claims that the senior men were discharged in order to circumvent the seniority clause. Surely the men should be reinstated if the truth of the allegation is proved. The requisite promise is implied, even though the contract says nothing about discharges, because a discharge for the purpose of circumventing seniority would destroy the right of employees to have the fruits of their bargain. Upon this familiar principle one might also fairly conclude in the absence of other evidence that the provisions of a collective bargaining agreement establishing

[29] Joerns Bros., Inc., 20 Lab. Arb. 715 (1953); A. D. Juilliard Co., 15 Lab. Arb. 934 (1951); Lawrence Prod. Co., 14 Lab. Arb. 310 (1950). *But see* Mosaic Tile Co., 13 Lab. Arb. 949 (1950).

[30] Another dramatic illustration is Remington Rand Co., 27 Lab. Arb. 880 (1956), award set aside, 27 Lab. Arb. 779 (N.Y. Sup. Ct. 1957).

[31] Gay & Co. v. Blanchard, 32 La. Ann. 497, 504 (1880); see RESTATEMENT, CONTRACTS § 315(1) (1932).

[32] *Cf.* Mastro Plastics Corp. v. NLRB, 350 U.S. 270 (1956).

[33] 3 WILLISTON, CONTRACTS § 570 (rev. ed. 1936).

wages and labor standards impliedly impose upon the employer an obligation not to seek a substitute labor supply at lower wages or inferior standards. The implied promise would, for example, prohibit subcontracting for this purpose.[34]

It is not clear in ordinary contract law whether these implied covenants rest upon a conclusion concerning the intent of the parties or a judicial notion of fairness and sound policy which supplies the obligation in the absence of some manifestation of a contrary intent. Probably there are elements of both. Many judicial and statutory rules of construction fill up gaps by formulating presumptions based upon notions of fairness and convenience mixed with an informed hunch as to the probable intention. Whatever the correct explanation, obviously something more is involved than determining the meaning of language, and this is true regardless of whether the source of the alleged right is a commercial contract or a collective bargaining agreement. In court this context is called the law of contracts. Arbitrators require a similar body of precepts in rendering their decisions.

5. These familiar aspects of the arbitrator's function under the standard grievance clause do not come within any literal meaning of the words "interpretation or application," although possibly one can stretch "application" far enough to include any claim ultimately traceable to a provision of the contract. However that may be, there is a fifth class of cases in which arbitrators adjudicate substantive rights which cannot be traced to any specific provision of the contract. Consider, for example, the familiar contract which reserves for management the right to direct the working force but forbids a discharge without just cause. Under such circumstances it is common practice for arbitrators to entertain grievances involving lesser discipline.[35] Many arbitrators have ruled that a labor agreement forbids discharge without just cause, even though the subject is not mentioned.[36] Again, suppose

[34] Some of the decisions holding that a contract impliedly restricts an employer's freedom to engage in subcontracting may be explained upon this ground, but others go beyond it. *E.g.*, Stockholders Pub. Co., 16 Lab. Arb. 644 (1951); Parke, Davis & Co., 15 Lab. Arb. 111 (1950); Celanese Corp. of America, 14 Lab. Arb. 31 (1950); Duquesne Light Co., 17 L.R.R.M. 2735 (1950); A. D. Juilliard Co., 21 Lab. Arb. 713 (1953). There are many court decisions and arbitration awards holding that subcontracting is a management function in the absence of some express restriction in the collective agreement. *E.g.*, Amalgamated Ass'n of St. Ry. Employees v. Greyhound Corp., 231 F.2d 585 (5th Cir. 1956); Allegheny Ludlum Steel Corp., 23 Lab. Arb. 171 (1954).

[35] *E.g.*, Commercial Pacific Cable Co., 111 Lab. Arb. 219 (1948).

[36] There is a conflict between arbitration awards upon the question and judicial decisions. *Compare* United Furniture Workers v. Little Rock Furniture Mfg. Co., 148 F. Supp. 129 (E.D. Ark 1957), *and* Held v. American Linen Supply Co., 6 Utah 2d

that a collective bargaining agreement stipulates that layoffs shall be made in reverse order of seniority and that the senior man shall be given preference in making transfers or promotions within the bargaining unit. The contract is silent with respect to overtime except that it provides premium pay for work in excess of eight hours a day or forty hours a week. A foreman distributes the available overtime work to a small group whom the other employees and the union claim are his favorites but whom the foreman calls the most efficient. Might not a grievance be sustained, claiming that overtime opportunities should be allocated in order of seniority? Certainly this would be the ruling if it had been the past practice to rely on seniority and the foreman was introducing a change.[87] In either case the arbitrator would be sustaining a claim not founded on the language of the contract but falling within its interstices and covered by rather plain implication.

V

The special characteristics which distinguish a collective bargaining agreement from the normal commercial contract explain why the process exemplified by the foregoing illustrations is the normal stuff of grievance arbitration.

One unique characteristic is the number of people affected and the complexity of their interests. The union often has interests of its own which may conflict with the claims of individuals because several classes of individuals may have divergent interests, because the demands of group organization and coherence clash with individual self-interest, or even because the union officialdom is not immediately responsive to wishes of a numerical majority of the members.

A collective agreement also covers a wide range of conduct and an enormous variety of problems. No state or federal statute, except possibly the tax laws, covers as wide a variety of subjects or impinges upon as many aspects of the ordinary company's business or a worker's life—wages, hours of employment, working conditions, health and accident insurance, retirement, pensions, promotions, layoffs, discipline, subcontracting, technological changes, workloads, and a host of minor items. Yet a collective bargaining agreement must also be kept short and simple enough for the ordinary worker to read and understand. Verbal incompleteness is inevitable; the meticulous detail of a cor-

---

106, 307 P.2d 210 (1957), *with* Pilot Freight Carriers, Inc., 22 Lab. Arb. 761 (1954), *and* Atwater Mfg. Co., 13 Lab. Arb. 747 (1949).

[87] See Corn Products Refining Co., 12 Lab. Arb. 389 (1949).

porate mortgage is unsuited to administration by ordinary workers. The details must be filled in outside of the words.

A labor contract operates prospectively over substantial periods. Nearly all run for at least one year. Many run for two or three years. The last basic steel contract was for three years and, although they are now shorter, the automobile contracts used to cover a five-year span. Not all commercial contracts, but surely those which are most familiar, relate to a single transaction—the conveyance of land, the sale of a horse, the assignment of a copyright. Since one can hardly foresee all the problems that will develop in an industrial establishment within even a single year, more scope must be left for creativeness in the course of performing the agreement.

The parties to collective agreements share a degree of mutual interdependence which we seldom associate with simple contracts. Sooner or later an employer and his employees must strike some kind of a bargain. The costs of disagreement are heavy. The pressure to reach an agreement is so great that the parties are often willing to contract although each knows that the other places a different meaning upon the words and they share only a common intent to postpone the issue and take a gamble upon an arbitrator's ruling if a decision is required. Sometimes the issue is simply ignored.

Once a contract is executed the pressure to maintain it is so great that the arbitrator can hardly acknowledge that since there was no meeting of the minds upon the question before him, there was no contract, and therefore the parties should go back and negotiate a solution. In one case, there was a three-week strike upon the question whether the new contract which the parties were negotiating should allow supervisors to assert seniority based on their total service with the company if a decline in production forced their demotion into the bargaining unit. The company demanded this stipulation. The union objected. The State Board of Conciliation and Arbitration suggested a new contract provision. The company's lawyer agreed to accept the proposal, provided that the record would show that the company understood the clause to give seniority to supervisors. The union's representatives also accepted the proposal but upon the stipulation that they understood the clause to deny seniority to supervisors. Later an arbitrator had to determine the meaning, although a court might have dismissed the case upon the ground that there was no meeting of the minds and therefore no agreement.[88]

[88] The illustration is drawn from personal experience.

One consequence of these four characteristics is that many provisions of the labor agreement must be expressed in general and flexible terms. The concept of "just cause" is an obvious illustration. Sometimes the negotiators can do no more than establish an appropriate set of procedures for resolving a class of problems; witness the provisions for fixing workloads and piece rates in many textile contracts. A collective agreement rarely expresses all the rights and duties falling within its scope. One cannot spell out every detail of life in an industrial establishment, or even that portion which both management and labor regard as matters of mutual concern. As Dean Shulman puts it:

> [The collective bargaining agreement] is not the "typical" offer and acceptance which normally is the basis for classroom or text discussions of contract law. It is not an undertaking to produce a specific result; indeed, it rarely speaks of the ultimate product. It is not made by parties who seek each other out to make a bargain from scratch and then each go his own way.... Though cast in an adversary position, both are dependent upon their common enterprise.... They meet in their contract negotiations to fix the terms and conditions of their collaboration in the future.[39]

The resulting contract is essentially an instrument of government, not merely an instrument of exchange. "The trade agreement thus becomes, as it were, the industrial constitution of the enterprise, setting forth the broad general principles upon which the relationship of employer and employee is to be conducted."[40]

One cannot reduce all the rules governing a community like an industrial plant to fifteen or even fifty pages. The institutional characteristics and governmental nature of the collective bargaining process demand a common law of the shop which implements and furnishes the context of the agreement. We must assume that intelligent negotiators acknowledged so plain a need unless they explicitly stated a contrary rule. Indeed, it is largely for these reasons that collective bargaining agreements provide their own administrative or judicial machinery—the ascending steps of the grievance procedure culminating in final and binding arbitration.

The process works with a measure of success because the contract is put down into a going enterprise which has evolved innumerable ways of doing things. To quote Dean Shulman once more:

> The parties to a collective bargaining agreement start in a going enterprise with a store of amorphous methods, attitudes, fears and problems.... [The contract] covers only a small part of their joint concern. It is based upon a mass of unstated assump-

[39] Address by Dean Shulman, *The Role of Arbitration in the Collective Bargaining Process,* in COLLECTIVE BARGAINING AND ARBITRATION 19, 20–21 (Institute of Industrial Relations, University of California 1949).

[40] NLRB v. Highland Park Mfg. Co., 110 F.2d 632, 638 (4th Cir. 1940).

tions and practices as to which the understanding of the parties may actually differ, and which it is wholly impractical to list in the agreement.[41]

This background not only gives meaning to the words of the instrument but is itself a source of contract rights.

The generalities, the deliberate ambiguities, the gaps, the unforeseen contingencies, and the need for a rule even though the agreement is silent all require a creativeness in contract administration which is quite unlike the attitude of one construing a deed, a promissory note, or a 300-page corporate trust indenture. The process of interpretation cannot be the same because the conditions that determine the character of the instruments are different. Until these basic institutional characteristics are recognized by the courts, the law will continue to play a destructive role in the administration of collective bargaining agreements.

One additional characteristic requires special emphasis. I have spoken of the collective bargaining agreement as an instrument of government because it regulates the diverse affairs of many people, with conflicting interests, over long periods of time. In the area covered by the contract management has yielded its ancient prerogative to a system of joint rule. Since management and labor are seldom agreed about the boundary line between the area to be brought under their joint regime and the area to be left to the unilateral control of management, the collective agreement is likely to be the product of conflicting aspirations. Sometimes the sphere of joint control is delineated, with all the rest reserved as management prerogatives. When such a stipulation appears, the arbitrator must enforce it ungrudgingly, for his function is to interpret the agreement. As often as not the impossibility of making an explicit compromise upon so touchy a question, coupled with the impossibility of not reaching an agreement, results in a more or less ambiguous silence. Then the agreement is an armed truce in a continuing struggle; yet the armistice line is not put upon the map.

The task of finding where the line would have been drawn if the parties who signed the contract had drawn it explicitly should be treated initially as a problem of interpretation within the jurisdiction of the arbitrator who is given power to decide questions concerning the interpretation and application of the agreement. For it is the agreement that draws the boundary line even though it does not draw it expressly. The interpreter must remember that the contract goes a distance but also that it stops, because it is a product of competing

[41] Address by Dean Shulman, *supra* note 39.

wills and its policy inheres as much in its limitations as in its affirmations. Nor is the interpreter left wholly without guidance. Even a vague management-functions clause suggests that the boundaries may be narrower than under a contract without it. Surely an open-ended arbitration clause indicates a wider area of joint sovereignty than a clause limiting the arbitrator to the interpretation and application of the contract. In a discharge case it would not be implausible to conclude, even if the contract is otherwise silent, that review of discharges to determine whether there is just cause is more consistent with a contract granting other forms of job security and industrial justice than is the reservation of untrammeled power to discharge for any reason which the employer deems sufficient. The plausibility is less, if indeed there is any, in the case of subcontracting or shift schedules.

It is wrong, therefore, for courts to assume as a premise for judicial reasoning upon the effect of a labor contract that management has freedom of action except as the union may point to some express limitation—wrong because it misconceives the nature of contract administration and wrong because it assumes as a premise for deductive reasoning the answer to a question which the management and labor of each business may have trouble resolving in principle and therefore leave for *ad hoc* disposition in the day-to-day process of living together. It is no answer to say that the parties can overturn the erroneous postulate by expressing themselves more clearly. Not only does such a rule put the burden upon the union, which seems unfair, but the very conditions I have sought to describe may preclude this solution.

VI

In addition to the task of fitting grievance arbitration into the surrounding legal system wherever management and labor have neglected the responsibility, the federal courts are charged with developing a body of substantive and procedural law governing rights and duties under collective bargaining agreements. Here again the path of the law will depend upon the willingness of judges to shape their decisions to the institutional needs of collective bargaining. Two examples will suffice to illustrate the proposition.

One of the major questions in the law of collective bargaining agreements is who may sue to enforce, or to settle, a claim based upon the contract, such as a claim to extra premiums for overtime employment.[42]

[42] I have discussed this problem at length in Cox, *Rights under a Labor Agreement*, 69 HARV. L. REV. 601 (1956). The above paragraphs are largely a distillation of the article cited.

In one view the legal relation between the employer, the union, and the employees is conceived as two bilateral contracts. One contract—between the employer and the union—is made up partly of promises running to the benefit of the union as an organization, like the checkoff or closed-shop clauses, and partly of provisions relating to wages, hours, and job security which the employer promises to incorporate in a second bilateral contract—the contract of hire between the employer and individual employees. Under this theory the union may sue for breach of the first contract but since it is not a party to the second contract, only the individual may sue for the breach of promises running to his benefit.[43] And since the claim for compensation is the individual's, it must follow that the union has no power to make a binding settlement.

A second theory holds that a collective bargaining agreement is a third-party contract with the employer as a promisor, the union as a promisee, and the employees as third-party beneficiaries.[44] In the *Westinghouse* case, Circuit Judge Staley argued that this description does not fit the facts because such promises as the union shop and checkoff do not benefit the individual workers,[45] but surely some of the promises in an instrument may run to the benefit of third parties while others benefit the promisee alone. The other objection to the third-party beneficiary theory—that the individual's labor is the sole consideration for the obligation to pay wages—is hardly an accurate description of the facts. In negotiating a collective agreement the employer promises a given wage scale as part of a package deal in return for various undertakings by the union including the promise not to strike, and it is rather unlikely that he would have agreed to the same wage scale without the union's promises. The individual's furnishing labor is a consideration, but not the only consideration, for the employer's promise to pay. Under this theory either the union or the employees may sue for breach of the promises inuring to the benefit of individual workers. When the individual sues, judgment may be entered for the amount due him. When the union sues, the decree may be for specific performance or the company can be required to pay the money into the registry of court for distribution to individual workers in supplementary proceedings. In a suit by either an individual or the union

[43] Ass'n of Westinghouse Salaried Employees v. Westinghouse Electric Corp., 210 F.2d 623 (3d Cir. 1954), *aff'd*, 348 U.S. 437 (1955).

[44] Leahy v. Smith, 137 Cal. App. 2d 884, 290 P.2d 679 (1955).

[45] 210 F.2d at 628.

alone, the judgment would not bind the absent party, but the employer could protect himself against a second suit by impleading the absent party.

Third, the legal situation under a collective bargaining agreement may be somewhat loosely compared to a trust with a chose in action as the res. In this view the bargaining representative, which is subject to fiduciary obligations, holds the employer's promises in trust for the benefit of the individuals. The trust is a common legal device for handling situations in which a single obligee is empowered to play a continuing role in the administration of contracts intended for the benefit of a large and ever changing group of beneficiaries who may have divergent interests. Massachusetts business trusts and mortgage indentures furnish familiar illustrations. According to this analogy the union would ordinarily be the only proper party to bring an action for breach of the collective agreement, and the judgment would bind the individuals. The union can enter into binding settlements with the employer. The individual's remedy is to show that the union's handling of the claim did not meet its fiduciary obligations.[46] In the latter case the individual could sue the union to compel it to perform its duties or he could join the union and the company as co-defendants and seek a judgment for the money alleged to be due him.

Such theories furnish tools of analysis. They help us to perceive the implications of particular issues—to see the relation between problems—so that we may achieve consistency and integrity instead of an illogical mass of *ad hoc* decisions. They remind us of the flexibility and adaptability of the common law. They become dangerous when artificially selected concepts are allowed to dictate the decision. Any of the three theories is a sound abstraction. In the final analysis one must deal with the underlying questions of policy which make one theory more appropriate than another. Logic cannot replace wisdom.

Thus we are led back to the institutional characteristics of a collective agreement, especially its governmental nature as a living, growing constitution. Individual workers would receive the most protection against arbitrary treatment under the theory that the provisions of a collective bargaining agreement relating to wages and hours become effective by incorporation into bilateral contracts of hire between the employer and each employee, but giving the union control over all claims arising under the collective agreement comports much better with its functional nature. Allowing an individual to carry a claim to

[46] Jenkins v. Wm. Schluderberg–T. J. Kurdle Co., 217 Md. 556, 144 A.2d 88 (1958).

arbitration whenever he is dissatisfied with the adjustment worked out by the company and the union treats issues that arise in the administration of a contract as if there were always a "right" interpretation to be divined from the instrument. It discourages the kind of day-to-day cooperation between company and union which is normally the mark of sound industrial relations—a dynamic human relationship in which grievances are treated as problems to be solved and contract clauses serve as guideposts. Because management and employees are involved in continuing relationships, their disposition of grievances and the arbitrator's rulings may become a body of subordinate rules for the future conduct of the enterprise. (I say "subordinate rules" because the contract may change them. They are rather like the judge-made law—the rubrics which the judges put upon statutes, the precepts which govern where the statute is silent, the context into which new bits of statutory law will be intruded.) When the interests of several groups conflict, or future needs run contrary to present desires, or when the individual's claim endangers group interests, the union's function is to resolve the competition by reaching an accommodation or striking a balance. The process is political. It involves a melange of power, numerical strength, mutual aid, reason, prejudice, and emotion. Limits must be placed on the authority of the group, but within the zone of fairness and rationality this method of self-government probably works better than the edicts of any outside tribunal.[47]

As a second example of the importance of giving effect to the institutional characteristics of labor agreements, consider the situation of a company which has discharged the union president for loafing in the washroom. The union immediately went on strike in plain violation of the contract, claiming that the president was discharged for his vigorous prosecution of grievances, but it now seeks to arbitrate the issue. May the company refuse to arbitrate, claiming that the union's breach of the no-strike clause gives the company the right to cancel the agreement? If I contract to buy fuel oil from a dealer who promises deliveries twenty-four hours a day as needed and he refuses to bring me oil on two or three cold nights in December, I may cancel the contract and buy my oil elsewhere without waiting all winter to see if he performs the rest of the contract. The element of bargain in a labor contract argues for the company's interpretation, for the no-strike pledge is the principal consideration which the company receives in exchange for

[47] The nature of the limits is discussed in Cox, *The Duty of Fair Representation*, 2 VILL. L. REV. 151 (1957).

its undertakings.[48] There are also opposing considerations. Collective agreements are negotiated for substantial periods after much travail. There are enormous pressures to reach agreement. Although the parties cannot go their separate ways, in the absence of the contract there will be no rules governing their joint endeavor. All these considerations argue that the company, although it could sue for any damage caused by the strike, should not be allowed to terminate the agreement.

Yet this is also an unhappy conclusion. The employer cannot sue the union for damages without creating resentment which will embitter future relations. Perhaps the law should devise a new doctrine more suited to industrial relations, under which the union, having violated its obligations in relation to the discharge, would be held to forfeit any rights in the same premises without disrupting other aspects of the collective bargaining relation.

VII

The nub of this chapter is very simple. Unless the law is once again to fail to meet the needs of men, the principles determining legal rights and duties under collective bargaining agreements should not be imposed by the courts from above because of precepts learned in other contexts; the governing principles must be drawn out of the institutions of labor relations and shaped to their needs.

This is the way in which our commercial law developed. Two and a half centuries ago Lord Mansfield took the customs and practices of the world of commerce—the law merchant—and incorporated them into the common law administered by courts of general jurisdiction. Perhaps a modern Mansfield may again demonstrate the creative talent of the common law by drawing upon industrial jurisprudence.

---

[48] This is the prevailing judicial opinion. See Marathon Electric Mfg. Co., 106 N.L.R.B. 1171 (1953), *aff'd,* 223 F.2d 338 (D.C. Cir. 1955); Boeing Airplane Co. v. Aeronautical Lodge No. 751, IAM, 188 F.2d 356 (9th Cir. 1951), *affirming* 91 F. Supp. 596 (W.D. Wash. 1950).

Chapter 5

The Public Interest in Internal Union Affairs

Labor organizations were established in an effort to solve wage earners' problems in an industrial community—to acquire greater bargaining power and job security, to extend the rule of law and gain a voice in industrial decisions. Later, the government encouraged unionization by guaranteeing workers the right to form, join, and assist labor organizations. The government also stimulated the growth of collective bargaining. Unions gained power partly by self-help and partly by law—some gained enormous power. Their officers are custodians of other people's money, who hold and disburse millions of dollars belonging to union members. No other private association has as much power over its members, for a union also exerts control over its members' livelihood and opportunities as well as the rules governing their daily lives. Under the National Labor Relations[1] and Railway Labor Acts[2] the union which acts as the bargaining representative has power, in conjunction with the employer, to fix a worker's wages, hours, and conditions of employment without his assent.[3] The individual employee may not lawfully negotiate with his employer.[4] As a matter of practice, and probably in legal theory, the union controls the grievance procedure through which contract rights are enforced.[5]

For a considerable period the national labor policy was focused upon the formation of unions and the operation of collective bargaining as

[1] 49 STAT. 449, as amended, 29 U.S.C. §§151–68 (1952).

[2] 45 U.S.C. ch. 8 (1952).

[3] See Steele v. Louisville & N.R.R., 323 U.S. 192, 202 (1944), in which Mr. Chief Justice Stone said on behalf of the Court, "Congress has seen fit to clothe the bargaining representative with powers comparable to those possessed by a legislative body both to create and restrict the rights of those whom it represents. . . ."

[4] Medo Photo Supply Co. v. NLRB, 321 U.S. 678 (1944); *cf.* J. I. Case Co. v. NLRB, 321 U.S. 332 (1944).

[5] For a recent decision indicating that the union has power to settle grievances see Jenkins v. Wm. Schluderberg–T. J. Kurdle Co., 217 Md. 556, 144 A.2d 88 (1958) (dictum). The point is discussed at length in Cox, *Rights Under a Labor Agreement*, 69 HARV. L. REV. 601 (1956).

a system of labor-management relations. The relationships between union officials and the organization and between the organization and its members were left to the realm of private law, administered by state courts, where labor unions were lumped in the general category of voluntary unincorporated associations together with churches, social clubs, and fraternal benefit associations.[6] As the wealth and power of labor unions increased, public attention was inevitably drawn to these internal relationships. They are federal problems because labor unions enjoy their present power chiefly by virtue of the National Labor Relations and Railway Labor Acts. John R. Commons pointed out as early as 1915:

> It has doubtless appealed to some people who consider the employer's position more powerful than that of the union, that the employer should be compelled in some way to deal with unions, or at least to confer with their representatives. But if the State recognizes any particular union by requiring the employer to recognize it, the State must necessarily guarantee the union to the extent that it must strip it of any abuses it may practice.[7]

Public concern about the internal affairs of labor unions began to be felt at the time of the Taft-Hartley debates in 1947, but the pressures did not become heavy until the McClellan Committee investigations a decade later. The pressure culminated in the enactment of the Labor Management Reporting and Disclosure Act of 1959.[8]

The task of public policy in this area is easily stated. It was important to build up the power of labor organizations as a counterpoise to the might of business corporations. It is important to maintain the unions' power. But the creation of institutions vested with power sufficient to fulfill their purposes also creates the danger that an institution may be erroneously supposed to have a value apart from its objectives, or may be used for the advantage of those who control it rather than for the benefit of those whom it was designed to serve. Public policy should minimize the danger without disabling the unions from performing their beneficent functions. The ability of labor organizations to bargain effectively with employers should not be impaired, for the unions' ability to advance the welfare of their members depends more upon effective bargaining than upon the conduct of union affairs. Care should also be taken not to weaken self-government in labor organizations.

---

[6] Chafee, *The Internal Affairs of Associations Not for Profit*, 43 HARV. L. REV. 993 (1930).

[7] U.S. Commission on Industrial Relations 374 (1915).

[8] Pub. L. No. 86–257, 86th Cong., 1st Sess. (Sept. 14, 1959), hereafter cited as LMRDA.

Little is gained if the state, in an effort to guarantee union democracy, imposes so rigid a system of public regulation that the members are unable to manage their own affairs.

For the purpose of applying these principles the interests of union members in the internal affairs of labor organizations can be divided along three useful, if somewhat artificial, lines:

1) the performance of the fiduciary obligations resting upon union officials, not only in handling money and carrying on the business of the organization but also in negotiating and administering collective bargaining agreements.

2) internal democracy, which means both control by the members and respect for the essential rights of individuals and minorities.

3) the preservation of individual freedom.

I

No argument is necessary to demonstrate that the large sums of money gathered into the treasuries of labor organizations belong to the members. The members are entitled to share in the management and expenditure of their funds, and to have a periodic accounting. The officers are fiduciaries charged with handling the funds for the benefit, and in accordance with the instructions, of the members. The McClellan Committee hearings demonstrated that important union officials were stealing from the members, chiefly in the International Union of Operating Engineers, the International Brotherhood of Teamsters, and the United Textile Workers. There could be no dispute about the desirability of stamping out the thievery and raising obstacles to its repetition. The only problem was to devise the most effective methods.

The Labor Management Reporting and Disclosure Act of 1959 pursues two courses. It creates new federal crimes in order to punish financial dishonesty on the part of union officials. Embezzlement of the funds of a labor organization engaged in an industry affecting commerce becomes a felony;[9] the willful destruction or falsification of its records is punishable as a misdemeanor.[10] Since the hearings uncovered large "loans" from union treasuries to union officials, which had not been repaid, the Act forbids lending an officer or member more than $2,000.[11] The prohibition may cause some inconvenience to international representatives transferred to new locations, for some unions previously lent them the capital necessary to resettle their families at

[9] LMRDA §501(c).

[10] LMRDA §209.

[11] LMRDA §503.

a low rate of interest, but the blanket prohibition is the only way to eliminate the use of loans to conceal embezzlement or to aid a dominant officer who wants capital for private speculation.

The LMRDA also requires every labor organization in an industry affecting interstate commerce to file an annual financial report disclosing its receipts and disbursements together with the sources and purposes thereof.[12] The reports are filed with the Secretary of Labor on forms prescribed by him. They are open to union members, the press, and the general public. A union is required to preserve the records necessary to verify and substantiate its reports.[13] The Secretary of Labor is authorized to investigate the accuracy of reports armed with the power to subpoena.[14] Failure to file a report or filing an intentionally false report is punishable by fine or imprisonment.[15]

The Secretary is also given the rather unusual power to "report to interested persons or officials concerning the facts required to be shown in any report required by this Act and concerning the reasons for failure or refusal to file such a report or any other matter which he deems to be appropriate as a result of such investigation."[16] This provision seeks to implement the basic theory of the statute—that the government should assure union members adequate information about the conduct of the union's financial affairs; that it should guarantee fair elections for the selection of officers; and that it should then trust the good sense of the members to remove any incompetent or dishonest officials. The Secretary's function is to furnish the members with the facts which should have been supplied by union officials. In legal usage "interested persons" means not the curious, but those who are substantially affected. Possibly the section permits an irresponsible Secretary to injure a union which displeases him by issuing hostile press releases without a hearing, but this is a power possessed by all prosecutors or investigators without express statutory authorization.[17] The risk is a small price to pay for the safeguard.

It remains to be seen whether the theory of reporting and disclosure will discourage the repetition of past scandals and eliminate honest but careless financial practices. Similar sanctions have proved sufficiently effective in other contexts to justify their use before resorting to harsher methods.

[12] LMRDA §201.
[13] LMRDA §§205–206, 209 (c).
[14] LMRDA §601.
[15] LMRDA §209.
[16] LMRDA §601.
[17] Glass v. Ickes, 117 F.2d 273 (D.C. Cir. 1940).

The preparation of reports will multiply paper work. The statute also requires each officer to obtain an individual bond.[18] It raises vague dangers of personal liability in the minds of men to whom legal proceedings are unfamiliar. Local union offices carry no pay and little honor. Thus the statute may make it harder to fill the necessary offices. Compliance with the bonding and reporting requirements will entail considerable expense. The easiest way for the international unions to meet these problems is to merge a number of locals into a single unit, a trend that was evident before the LMRDA was enacted. Since there was no evidence of past misconduct and little temptation to dishonesty in truly small unions, the Senate sought to minimize the problem by creating a revocable exemption in their case,[19] but the coalition of Republicans and Southern Democrats insisted upon deleting the exemption in order to "toughen" the bill. There remains a provision authorizing the Secretary of Labor to provide a simplified form of report for small locals.[20] The Secretary and his advisers will be subject to heavy pressure to be cautious and require detailed reports lest they be criticized if wrongdoing occurs in a local union authorized to use the simplified form. Imaginative and courageous use of the discretionary power would overcome the greater danger of crushing small locals by burdensome reports.

More disturbing than the outright thievery revealed by the McClellan Committee was the evidence of the use of union office for personal profit, for one suspects that the vice of playing both sides of the street, under-cover deals, and conflicts of interest infect a good many unions whose officials believe themselves to be personally honest. Two illustrations reported by the committee deserve mention. About 1950 Peter W. Weber, business manager of Local 825 of the International Union of Operating Engineers, secured a 12 per cent interest in Public Constructors, Inc., in exchange for a loan of $2,500. Public Constructors did business within the territorial jurisdiction of Local 825 and had collective bargaining agreements with that union. In the negotiation and administration of these contracts Weber's personal financial interests stood in direct conflict with unselfish devotion to the welfare of the employees. By 1957 the book value of his business interest had increased to almost fifty times its cost—to $108,677.[21] Other evidence

[18] LMRDA §502.

[19] S. 1555, 86th Cong., 1st Sess., as passed by Senate, §201(d).

[20] LMRDA §208. After this lecture had been delivered the text of the Secretary's order prescribing forms of reports became available. 29 C.F.R. pt. 403, §§403.1–403.10. The simplified form for small unions appears to minimize the difficulties of reporting.

[21] *Hearings Before the Select Committee on Improper Activities in the Labor or Management Field,* 85th Cong., 1st Sess., pt. 20, 8134–40 (1958).

tended to show that James Hoffa held interests in firms with which the International Brotherhood of Teamsters bargained.[22]

Such conduct offends ancient moral precepts. The common law has condemned it for generations. AFL-CIO Ethical Practices Code IV states that "a basic ethical principle in the conduct of union affairs is that no responsible trade union official should have a personal financial interest which conflicts with the full performance of his fiduciary duties as a workers' representative." The code then condemns a number of specific practices illustrating the basic principle: loans by a union to an officer, owning an interest in a business with which the union bargains or in an enterprise which is in competition with such a business, and owning an interest in an enterprise a substantial part of which consists of buying from, selling to, or otherwise dealing with a business with which the union bargains.

Unfortunately the AFL-CIO lacks power to implement the code except by expelling an entire international union. It has no method of gathering evidence. It cannot proceed against individuals. In many cases the sanction of expulsion would be too severe, in others too harmful to the labor movement.

The original Kennedy bills sought to support the underlying moral precepts by requiring every union officer annually to report to the Secretary of Labor any holdings, income, or transactions which created a potential conflict between his personal interests and loyalty to the members.[23] These sections, which reach not only cases where the official has legal title, but also beneficial ownership held through "covers," "straws," or "blinds," were carried into the LMRDA without amendment.[24] True criminals will undoubtedly ignore the duty to report, but the detailed and unequivocal legislative condemnation of specific holdings and transactions should go far toward establishing a higher standard of conduct. The official whose fingers itch for a "fast buck" but who is not a criminal will be deterred by the fear of prosecution if he files no report and by fear of reprisal from the members if he does.

Despite the scarcity of direct precedent, it seems plain that all union officers and employees have always been subject to the usual common-law fiduciary duties of an agent.[25] Violations are redressible in the state

[22] *Ibid.*, pt. 13, 5038 (1957).

[23] S. 3454, 85th Cong., 2d Sess. §102.

[24] LMRDA §202.

[25] Union officers are obviously agents. All true agents owe fiduciary obligations to their principals. RESTATEMENT (SECOND), AGENCY §§13, 387–98. Curiously, there appear to be only two judicial opinions which set forth the rule. Dusing v. Nuzzo, 26 N.Y.S.2d 345 (N.Y. Sup. Ct. 1941); Tinkler v. Powell, 23 Wyo. 352, 151 Pac. 1097 (1915).

courts. The duty is so seldom enforced, however, that the House Labor Committee adopted, and the Senate approved, an amendment giving it a federal statutory base. Section 501(a) states in general terms the union agent's obligation to act solely for the benefit of his principal, to be loyal, to refrain from competing with his principal or acquiring conflicting interests, and "to account . . . for any profits received by him in whatever capacity in connection with transactions conducted by him or under his direction." The principles stated in Section 501(a) were drawn from the Restatement of Agency in an effort to incorporate the whole body of common-law precedents defining the fiduciary obligations of agents and trustees[26] with such adaptations as might be required to take into account "the special problems and functions of a labor organization."[27]

Section 501(b) authorizes any union member to bring a suit in the federal court in the nature of a minority stockholder's suit whenever his union refuses to sue an officer or employee alleged to be guilty of a breach of fiduciary obligations. The trial judge may allot part of any sums recoverable for counsel fees and expenses. All the usual remedies for breach of trust are available.[28]

These provisions are potentially among the most important in the LMRDA. If individual members have the initiative and interest to bring suit, the Becks, Hoffas, and Webers may be required to account not only for any misappropriations but also for all the profits which they have made by virtue of their offices. Equity would impose a trust for the benefit of the Operating Engineers upon Weber's stock in Public Constructors, if the findings of the McClellan Committee were sustained in court. Beck would be required to account for the monies or gifts received from Nathan Shefferman. If Hoffa received loans from the Teamsters, he might well be required to account not only for the money but also for any proceeds of his investment.

Section 501 imposes no restrictions upon the purposes for which a labor organization may expend its funds. The propriety of union activities other than collective bargaining, such as charitable contributions and support for political candidates, may be fairly debatable, but this is a separate issue of too great importance for the courts to resolve by interpreting a provision which deals directly with only the duties of

[26] See RESTATEMENT (SECOND), AGENCY §§387, 388, 389, 394, from which the language of LMRDA §501(a) was derived.

[27] LMRDA §501(a).

[28] LMRDA §501(b) provides that the action may be brought "to recover damages or secure an accounting or other appropriate relief."

union agents to the organization and its members. Read in their context the words are plain; it is made the duty of the union officers and agents "to manage, invest, and expend [the union's money and property] in accordance with its constitution and by-laws and any resolutions of the governing bodies adopted thereunder." An agent who follows the instructions of his principal is not guilty of a breach of fiduciary duties. Section 501 emphasizes the importance of giving careful attention to the constitutional provisions and resolutions of governing bodies, but where the union grants the necessary authority, no statutory restriction is imposed. If there were ambiguity it would be dispelled by the statement of five members of the House Labor Committee in reporting the committee bill, for they were the five who sponsored the bill and they included Congressman O'Hara, who proposed Section 501 in the Labor Committee. Senator Kennedy gave a similar explanation in presenting the Conference Report.[29]

II

In a rudimentary modern political sense democracy implies (a) control of governing decisions by those affected, and (b) a decent respect for the fundamental rights of individuals and minorities, not only by the individuals in power but also by the ruling majority. No politician dares publicly to question the value of democracy in labor organizations but a quiet and serious debate is, nevertheless, in progress. According to one view, labor unions should be regarded as military organizations, for their function is to wage economic warfare with employers who are constantly feeling out chinks in the unions' defenses through which to wound if not destroy them. As a wartime army can neither brook divided leadership nor tolerate active dissidents, so must a union punish the troublemakers in order to close ranks against employers and rival organizations. The sophisticated exponents of this view also contend that since union officials have better training and more experience than the rank-and-file members, those officials who are given the power will act more responsibly in enforcing the union's obligations to employers, will present fewer preposterous or impractical demands, and, if allowed the power, will enforce their decisions. Professor John T. Dunlop warns us:

> Already we are seeing employers who urged Congress to pass "strong legislation" affecting internal union government going to national union officers as of old seeking national union support to restrain the demands of locals and to make agreements.

[29] H.R. Rep. No. 741, 86th Cong., 1st Sess. 81–82; 105 Cong. Rec. 1433 (daily ed. Sept. 3, 1959).

They are not likely to get as much cooperation; they could not be given as much. The country has chosen on the grounds of morality and democracy to make wage stability more difficult to achieve.[80]

The advocates of this position hope to improve union government by creating a sense of professional responsibility among union officials. Perhaps the partial professionalization of management is an encouraging precedent.

Yet the argument is hardly persuasive. An autocratic union may serve the material demands of its members by bargaining effectively for higher wages and increased benefits. It may establish a measure of job security. None except a democratic union, however, can achieve the idealistic aspirations that justify labor organizations. Collective bargaining may limit the employer's power by substituting a negotiated agreement for arbitrary tyranny of the boss, but it scarcely extends the rule of law to substitute an autocratic union. Only in a democratic union can workers, through chosen representatives, participate jointly with management in the government of their industrial lives, even as all of us may participate, through elected representatives, in political government.

The state alone cannot achieve true union democracy but it has much to contribute. Preserving democracy requires protecting individuals and minorities against numerical majorities or an officialdom which acts with the majority's consent. It is not enough to put our trust in self-restraint. The task of assuring workers the ultimate control of the affairs of their unions should be undertaken by law because it is the law which gives a union, as bargaining representative, the quasi-legislative power to bind employees in the bargaining unit without their consent.

Half a century ago unions were too fragile to survive internal dissension, but surely no one seriously doubts the current ability of the major labor organizations to survive free elections, free debate, and a decent respect for minorities among the members. To show that union officials have a better grasp of economic policy than the rank and file, and a higher sense of obligation, does not demonstrate the wisdom of aristocratic government in labor relations for the same reasons that the parallel argument fails in relation to the government of nations. Leadership is required, but it should be achieved by the arts of the statesman and not by the easy road of compulsion with its denials of opportunity and temptations to tyranny and sloth. The

[80] *Hearings Before the Joint Committee upon the Economic Report,* 86th Cong., 2d Sess. (1959).

proper balance between control by the membership and the executive direction necessary to effective action cannot be achieved by general debate about the desirability of democracy; it involves specific questions concerning the disposition of power and the frequency of elections.[31]

Union Membership. Union practices pertaining to the admission and expulsion of members are the threshold to democracy in the government of labor organizations. An employee in a bargaining unit who is unfairly excluded from the union which represents the unit or who is unjustly expelled from membership has no opportunity to participate in fixing the terms and conditions of his employment. He is bound by the action of an organization in whose councils he has no voice. In his case it is a fraud to call collective bargaining an instrument of industrial democracy. Expulsion may be used as a method of suppressing criticism or destroying political opposition. Furthermore, quite apart from problems of union government, control over membership may be used to restrict individual liberty, for example, where members are disciplined because of activities in state or national politics distasteful to union officials.

Although the legal rules were originally formulated in cases involving religious organizations, social clubs, and, somewhat later, fraternal benefit associations, the courts have evolved satisfactory rules applicable to the expulsion of union members.[32] Upon the theory that improper expulsion violates the member's interest in the organization's property or a contract between him and the other members made up of the constitution and bylaws or, in recent years, upon the ground that there is a tortious interference with an advantageous relationship, the courts will set aside an expulsion upon any of five grounds:

1. The procedure violated the union's constitution or bylaws.[33]

2. The constitution or bylaws did not authorize expulsion for the alleged offense.[34]

3. The procedure, though it conformed to the union's constitution and bylaws, did not afford the member a fair hearing.[35]

---

[31] See pp. 99–102 *infra*.

[32] The best discussion is Summers, *Legal Limitations on Union Discipline*, 64 HARV. L. REV. 1049 (1951).

[33] Harris v. National Union of Marine Cooks, 98 Cal. App. 2d 733, 221 P.2d 136 (Dist. Ct. App. 1950); Walsh v. Reardon, 274 Mass. 530, 174 N.E. 912 (1931); Howland v. Local 306, UAW–CIO, 323 Mich. 305, 35 N.W.2d 166 (1948); Savard v. Industrial Trades Union of America, 76 R.I. 496, 72 A.2d 660 (1950).

[34] Otto v. Journeymen Tailors' Union, 75 Cal. 308, 17 Pac. 217 (1888).

[35] Gilmore v. Palmer, 109 Misc. 552, 179 N.Y. Supp. 1 (Sup. Ct. 1919). *Contra*, State *ex rel.* Dame v. Le Fevre, 251 Wis. 146, 28 N.W.2d 349 (1947).

4. The expulsion, though it was authorized by the union's constitution and bylaws, was "unreasonable," contrary to "public policy," or contrary to "natural justice."[36]

5. The expulsion was in bad faith because the purported ground was only a pretense for getting rid of a troublesome member.[37]

The rule invalidating expulsion without a hearing requires observance of much the same minimum safeguards as the due process clause of the Fifth and Fourteenth Amendments has been held to impose upon the adjudicative procedures of the state and federal governments. The accused member must be given an opportunity to hear the charge,[38] to present evidence in his defense,[39] and to confront and probably to cross-examine the witnesses against him.[40] Any special trial body may not include his accusers,[41] but presumably a trial may be held before the full membership. It seems unlikely that the accused member is entitled to the aid of a lawyer in his defense. The accused is entitled to be put upon a roughly equal footing with the prosecutors. If they are laymen, surely he is entitled to no more professional assistance. Although the union officers, who are likely to be behind the prosecutors, are usually more skilled than ordinary members in the rules of procedure, turning a trial over to professional advocates would entail disproportionate loss in self-government.

The common law grew more slowly in pricking out the line between permissible grounds of expulsion and grounds which are inadequate despite the authority in the constitution or bylaws. A member may be

[36] See Swaine v. Miller, 72 Mo. App. 444, 446 (1897); Spayd v. Ringing Rock Lodge No. 665, Bhd. of R.R. Trainmen, 270 Pa. 67, 113 Atl. 70 (1921); Chafee, *supra* note 6, at 1015–18; *cf.* Dawkins v. Antrobus, 44 L.T.R. (n.s.) 557, 559–60 (C.A. 1881) (dictum).

[37] Otto v. Journeymen Tailors' Union, 75 Cal. 308, 17 Pac. 217 (1888); Fleming v. Moving Picture Mach. Operators, 16 N.J. Misc. 502, 1 A.2d 850 (Ch. 1938), *aff'd*, 124 N.J. Eq. 269, 1 A.2d 386 (Ct. Err. & App. 1939); Kuzych v. White, [1950] 4 D.L.R. 187 (B.C. Ct. App.), *cf.* Eschman v. Huebner, 226 Ill. App. 537 (1922).

[38] Armant v. Cannon Employees, 11 L.R.R.M. 752 (Cal. Super. Ct. 1942) (member not informed of evidence against him); Walsh v. International Alliance of Theatrical Stage Employees, 22 N.J. Misc. 161, 37 A.2d 667 (Ch. 1944) (charge too vague); Bartone v. Di Pietro, 18 N.Y.S.2d 178 (Sup. Ct. 1939) (no notice of nature of charge).

[39] Cotton Jammers' Ass'n v. Taylor, 23 Tex. Civ. App. 367, 56 S.W. 553 (Civ. App. 1900) (alternative holding).

[40] Armant v. Cannon Employees, 11 L.R.R.M. 752 (Cal. Super. Ct. 1942); Brooks v. Engar, 259 App. Div. 333, 19 N.Y.S.2d 114, *appeal dismissed mem.*, 284 N.Y. 767, 31 N.E.2d 514 (1940); Fales v. Musicians' Protective Union, 40 R.I. 34, 99 Atl. 823 (1917).

[41] Gaestel v. Brotherhood of Painters, 120 N.J. Eq. 358, 185 Atl. 36 (Ch. 1936); Coleman v. O'Leary, 58 N.Y.S.2d 812 (Sup. Ct.) (alternative holding), *appeal dismissed as moot mem.*, 269 App. Div. 972, 58 N.Y.S.2d 358 (1945); *cf.* Cohen v. Rosenburg, 262 App. Div. 274, 27 N.Y.S.2d 834 (1941), *aff'd per curiam*, 287 N.Y. 800, 40 N.E.2d 1018 (1942).

expelled for strikebreaking,[42] for working at wages below the union scale,[43] or for aiding an employer to obtain an injunction against a strike.[44] But a member of a licensing board cannot be lawfully expelled by his union because his official actions displease it,[45] nor may a union expel a member for testifying against it under oath in an arbitration proceeding.[46] The familiar provision in union constitutions which states that bringing suit against the union is cause for expulsion is plainly invalid.[47] There is a nice factual line to be drawn between legitimate criticism, which as an exercise of the privilege of free speech will not justify expulsion, and stirring up dissension within the union, which is a justification.[48] The most difficult issues involve the right of a union to control its members' activities in fields outside the sphere of collective bargaining but vitally important to the welfare of its members.[49]

The LMRDA adds little to the existing law. The Senate Labor Committee decided not to recommend legislation protecting union membership. The amendments added on the floor dealt with the subject haphazardly. Section 101 (a) (5) incorporates into the federal statute the existing common law prohibiting the suspension or discipline of a union member except for nonpayment of dues "unless such member has been (A) served with written specific charges; (B) given a reasonable time to prepare his defense; (C) afforded a full and fair hearing." Section 101 (a) (4) probably forbids discipline for bringing suit against a union.[50] Section 609 forbids punishing a member "for exercising any right to which he is entitled under the provisions of this Act."

[42] Becker v. Calnan, 313 Mass. 625, 48 N.E.2d 668 (1943); Havens v. King, 221 App. Div. 475, 224 N.Y. Supp. 193 (1927), *aff'd per curiam sub nom.* Havens v. Dodge, 250 N.Y. 617, 166 N.E. 346 (1929).

[43] *Cf.* O'Keefe v. Local 463, United Ass'n of Plumbers, 277 N.Y. 300, 14 N.E.2d 77 (1938); Schmidt v. Rosenburg, 49 N.Y.S.2d 364 (Sup. Ct. 1944), *aff'd mem.,* 269 App. Div. 685, 54 N.Y.S.2d 379 (1945).

[44] Burke v. Monumental Div., No. 52, Bhd. of Locomotive Eng'rs, 286 Fed. 949 (D. Md. 1922), *aff'd per curiam,* 298 Fed. 1019 (4th Cir 1924), *rev'd per curiam on other grounds,* 270 U.S. 629 (1926).

[45] Schneider v. Local 60, United Ass'n Journeymen Plumbers, 116 La. 270, 40 So. 700 (1905).

[46] *Cf.* Angrisani v. Stearn, 167 Misc. 731, 3 N.Y.S.2d 701 (Sup. Ct. 1938), *aff'd mem.,* 255 App. Div. 975, 8 N.Y.S.2d 997 (1939); Thompson v. Grand Int'l Bhd. of Locomotive Eng'rs, 41 Tex. Civ. App. 176, 91 S.W. 834 (Civ. App. 1905); Link-Belt Speeder Corp., 2 Lab. Arb. 338 (1945).

[47] Burke v. Monumental Div., No. 52, Bhd. of Locomotive Eng'rs, 273 Fed. 707 (D. Md. 1919); see Trailmobile Co. v. Whirls, 331 U.S. 40, 69 (1947) (Jackson, J., dissenting).

[48] See Summers, *Legal Limitations on Union Discipline,* 64 HARV. L. REV. 1049, 1069–71, 1074 (1951).

[49] See pp. 106–111 *infra.*

[50] See pp. 103–106 *infra.*

No useful purpose is served by these provisions, unless it be to publicize the availability of remedies. No additional substantive law was required, and none was created. The need was for a more practical remedy than suit by an individual employee. Congress failed to provide one. Since the federal provisions do not exclude state law,[51] their principal consequence will be technical jurisdictional difficulties. Violations of the federal statute are actionable in the district courts of the United States.[52] In other cases improper discipline will give rise only to a state cause of action. If a member sues in the federal court alleging that he was disciplined without a fair hearing but proves only that the discipline was for a cause unauthorized by the union constitution or bylaws, must his suit be dismissed for want of jurisdiction? Or may state and federal causes of action be joined under the doctrine of pendant jurisdiction in the manner of an action for statutory trademark infringement and common-law unfair competition? Probably there is pendant jurisdiction if the federal cause of action is not frivolous.[53]

Admission. Congress also failed to provide new substantive law in the one field in which it was urgently needed—the admission of members. It is a black-letter rule that no one has a legally protected right to become a member of a voluntary association.[54] Consequently, a union may exclude an applicant for any reason, good or bad, or for no reason. It may even discriminate upon grounds of race, color, sex, or religion.

Until recently there was reason to hope that the courts might gradually change the rule applicable to labor unions. Its repetition gives it a stronger ring of authority than the direct precedents warrant. Union membership rarely involves the close personal association which must have influenced the courts in their refusal to compel social clubs to admit unwanted members, nor does eligibility turn upon the theological niceties pertinent to religious organizations. Unions exercise powers under the National Labor Relations and Railway Labor Acts which are far greater than the power of other voluntary associations—greater indeed than the powers which unions exercised prior to the legislation. Since union membership is correspondingly more important, this factor was ample ground for distinguishing the earlier cases and recog-

[51] LMRDA §103.

[52] LMRDA §102.

[53] Hurn v. Ousler, 289 U.S. 238 (1933); HART & WECHSLER, THE FEDERAL COURTS AND THE FEDERAL SYSTEM 797–809 (1953).

[54] 87 C.J.S. *Trade Unions* §33 (1954). But the modern view denies a union the privilege of enforcing closed-shop contracts against those to whom it has arbitrarily denied admission. See James v. Marinship Corp., 25 Cal. 2d 721, 155 P.2d 329 (1945).

nizing a legally protected interest in a fair opportunity to become a member of the union which acts as the bargaining representative of the unit in which the applicant is employed.[55] It was also possible to argue that performance of the representative's duty of fair representation requires admitting all members of the bargaining unit to union membership, in the absence of proper cause for exclusion, because membership is the best assurance that the employee's voice will be heard and his interests be represented. Unfortunately, the decision in *Ross v. Ebert*[56] and the Supreme Court's refusal to review the *Oliphant* case[57] have discouraged, if not permanently foreclosed, this avenue of progress.

The prospect for federal legislation is also dim. Unions oppose it partly because of a belief that absolute freedom to select members is the right of a voluntary association and partly upon the practical ground that forced integration would prevent the unionization of southern workers. Congressmen from the southern states oppose such legislation as part of the battle over segregation. The combination is unbeatable.

As a practical matter, therefore, protection of the public interest in affording employees an opportunity to participate in the affairs of the unions which represent them rests in the hands of the labor movement. If the AFL-CIO would take stronger measures to press its affiliates to conform to its constitutional provisions against discrimination,[58] it might well find that the gains from a revival of conscience offset any immediate practical loss.

Union Elections. The election of officers is the heart of union democracy. The policies of any large organization must be formulated and administered by a small group of officials. Their responsiveness to the members depends upon the frequency of elections, a fair opportunity to nominate and vote for candidates, and an honest count of the ballots.

Commentators are in disagreement as to the capacity of the common law to police the electoral process in labor organizations.[59] A court can

[55] *Cf.* Dusing v. Nuzzo, 177 Misc. 35, 37, 29 N.Y.S.2d 882, 884 (Sup. Ct. 1941), *modified*, 263 App. Div. 59, 31 N.Y.S.2d 849 (1941); Raevsky v. Upholsterers' Int'l Union, 38 Pa. D. & C. 187, 195 (C.P. 1940).

[56] 275 Wisc. 523, 82 N.W.2d 315 (1957).

[57] Oliphant v. Brotherhood of Locomotive Firemen, 156 F. Supp. 89 (N.D. Ohio 1957), *cert. denied*, 355 U.S. 893 (1957), *aff'd*, 262 F.2d 359 (6th Cir. 1958), *cert. denied*, 359 U.S. 935 (1959).

[58] Art. II, §4.

[59] *Compare* Wellington, *Union Democracy and Fair Representation*, 67 YALE L.J. 1327, 1347–49 (1958), *with* Cox, *The Role of Law in Preserving Union Democracy*, 72 HARV. L. REV. 609, 624–29 (1959).

undoubtedly grant effective relief against violations of a union's own constitutions and bylaws, except where foreclosed by doctrinal rulings requiring the violation of a property right, but it would be hard for the court to supervise elections and virtually impossible to supply the minimum electoral guarantees if they were missing from the union's constitution.

The LMRDA establishes comprehensive requirements for the conduct of union elections. Local officers must be elected every three years or oftener by secret ballot of the members or by a convention chosen by secret ballot.[60] International officers must be elected every five years or oftener by a secret ballot of the members or by a convention of delegates chosen by secret ballot.[61] There are appropriate guarantees of the right to nominate and support candidates, to run for office, to get written notice of the election, and to vote without "improper interference or reprisal of any kind."[62] Every member is guaranteed one vote, a provision which not only invalidates the practice of limiting the vote to a special class of members but which also assures apprentices and even employers a voice in the selection of the officers of any labor organization to which they may belong. The statute assures honest elections by giving each candidate the right to have an observer at the polls and at the counting of the ballots, and by requiring separate publication of the results of the balloting in each local union. The latter requirement is pertinent to international elections. The division of sentiment in a single local is usually well enough known to its members to reveal any serious dishonesty in counting the ballots, provided that the figures are not concealed by lumping them into a single total with the results in other local unions. The Act makes compliance with the union's constitution and bylaws a statutory obligation in order that a federal remedy may be available for violations.[63]

To prevent union officials from gaining improper advantage in union elections Section 401 (e) requires the union to distribute any candidate's campaign literature at his expense and to refrain from discrimination between candidates. Section 401 (g) prohibits using union funds to promote the candidacy of any person. The administration of the latter provision will require delicate judgments. When a union president visits major locals on union business during the months before an election, he is not unmindful of his political fences. The international

[60] LMRDA §401(b).
[61] LMRDA §401(a).
[62] LMRDA §401(e).
[63] LMRDA §§401(e) and (f).

representative who goes to another city to handle grievances may be expected to discuss an impending election. The incumbents invariably command more space in the union newspaper than the opposition. Legislation can no more wipe out these advantages than it can prevent a President's dramatic move toward world peace from aiding his campaign for re-election. The statute should help to eliminate such grossly unfair tactics as hiring additional organizers to campaign for the re-election of incumbent officials or using the union treasury to send out election propaganda.

The demand that all candidates be given access to the union's membership list produced sharp debate in Congress because two irreconcilable principles were at stake. Since a candidate seeking to defeat the incumbent would be seriously hampered by the lack of a voting list, access to membership lists became a symbol of truly democratic elections in the eyes of those congressmen who would not count it a loss if labor unions were damaged in the process. On the other hand, the unions attach great importance to the secrecy of their membership lists because employers, rival unions, and subversive organizations have often used the lists for improper purposes. Under present conditions the need for secrecy is probably exaggerated, but one friendly to the labor movement could hardly ignore the strength of the tradition or the force of experience even though he was also driven to acknowledge that the preservation of secrecy diminished the fairness of the election. In the end a compromise was reached which gives a candidate the right to inspect a list of members who are employed under union security contracts, once within thirty days of the election and without copying the list. This limited privilege can hardly be abused.[64]

Enforcement of the election requirements is vested in the Secretary of Labor. A member desiring to challenge an election must first invoke his remedies within the organization. After they are exhausted or if three months elapse without a decision, he may file a complaint with the Secretary who, upon investigation, will either dismiss the complaint or file an action in the federal court to set aside the election. The complaint is to be upheld only if it appears that the violation of the statute "may have affected the outcome of the election."[65] It would be wasteful to set aside an election for violations which could not have affected the result, but obviously proof that the outcome would have been different is not required. If an election is set aside, the Secretary is to conduct a new election.[66]

[64] LMRDA §401(c).
[65] LMRDA §402(c).
[66] *Ibid.*

The foregoing provisions seem adequate to guarantee free and fair union elections. They descend too far into detail, sacrificing the ideal of self-government, but there is no requirement which can seriously hamper a union's normal functioning. Only the requirement of individual notice of elections on stated occasions can be criticized as expensive,[67] and the cost is certainly no more than 10 cents a member for each election.

Participation in Union Affairs. Section 101 (a) of the LMRDA guarantees all union members "equal rights and privileges" in nominating candidates and voting in union elections, in attending union meetings, and in discussing and voting upon union affairs, all "subject to reasonable rules and regulations in such organization's constitution and bylaws." The qualification is the result of a compromise between the practicalities of union government and the commendable aim of preventing unjust discrimination between union members. Time and litigation will be required to determine what are "reasonable rules and regulations," but the basic distinction is not hard to illustrate. Many local unions have a mixed membership. A local of the International Brotherhood of Electrical Workers, for example, may include construction workers and also members from a power company or a manufacturing concern. If the business on the agenda were whether to strike or ratify a proposed contract covering electrical construction, it would not be unreasonable to bar the industrial members from the vote. If a local industrial union had members from four noncompetitive factories, it would be reasonable to provide in the bylaws that only the members employed at a company should vote upon items of business confined to their bargaining unit. To have outlawed such bylaws would have unnecessarily curtailed the principle of self-determination. On the other hand, Section 101 (a) (1) unquestionably bans classifications of voting and nonvoting members such as existed in the International Union of Operating Engineers.[68]

Discrimination against apprentices is probably unreasonable, although the distinction has the possible justification that they are usually less mature than journeymen members while they are learning the trade. The Culinary Workers, Barbers, and other unions which admit employers to membership will probably have to choose, when subject to the Act, between granting employers the right to participate in meetings, which has heretofore been denied, and surrendering this method

[67] LMRDA §401(e).

[68] Interim Report of the Select Committee on Improper Activities in the Labor or Management Field, S. Rep. No. 1417, 85th Cong., 2d Sess. 437 (1958).

of subjecting employers to the union's rules. The principle underlying Section 101 (a) (1) is that those who are bound, as members, by the union's decision should have part in the deliberations. All members are plainly entitled to vote in union elections, for the statutory right of each member to cast one vote cannot be qualified by even a reasonable rule.[69]

Some unions allow retired employees and workers who have left the trade or industry to retain their cards as nonvoting members. Surely this is reasonable in substance, but the doubt would be reduced by constitutional amendments establishing a special category of members emeriti who, like retired professors, would retain the dignity and social status of members but lose the rights and duties.

Section 101 (a) (1) may also help to check the use of violence to suppress dissent, which every student of union government knows to occur even though he cannot document the assertion. To evict a dissident from a meeting would violate Section 101 (a) (1) unless he violated normal rules of decorum. Section 101 (a) (2) carries the legal protection a step further by guaranteeing freedom of speech inside and outside union meetings, and also by securing the critics an opportunity to meet for the purpose of organizing their opposition. The latter privilege would seem essential to effective minorities even though it flies in the face of traditional trade-union opposition to any form of caucus or separate assemblage. However, dissent in a union, like treason within a nation, can be lawfully suppressed if the purpose is to destroy the union or encourage a rival.[70]

Right to Sue. At common law the rights of individual members can be enforced only by individual suits; the initiative and costs necessary for prosecution must come from the member. The LMRDA preserves this condition except that the election and trusteeship titles are enforceable by the Secretary of Labor upon the complaint of a member.[71] Section 101 (a) (4) grants additional protection for this right, but its meaning is obscure because the draftsman failed to distinguish two radically different kinds of limitations upon a union member's freedom to sue the organization.

One limitation is the familiar provision in union constitutions which

---

[69] LMRDA §402(e).

[70] Section 101(a)(2) permits a union to qualify the rights of freedom of speech and assembly by "reasonable rules as to the responsibility of every member towards the organization as an institution and to his refraining from conduct that would interfere with its performance of its legal or contractual obligations.

[71] LMRDA §§304 and 402.

forbids suit against the union under penalty of discipline unless the member has exhausted his internal remedies.[72] This clause should be void as against public policy. No private organization should be permitted to restrict any person's access to courts of justice. This right should be as absolute as the right to appear in court as a witness, to petition a legislature, or to communicate with a member of Congress.[73]

A quite different kind of limitation is imposed by the judicial doctrine that a court will not entertain a member's action against a labor organization until he has exhausted all adequate remedies within the organization. The rule is one of judicial administration. It applies not only to suits involving the internal affairs of all forms of voluntary association[74] but also to actions upon ordinary contracts, including collective bargaining agreements.[75] In an exaggerated form the exhaustion-of-remedies doctrine may deny legal relief to a plaintiff whose internal remedy is vain, too slow, or too expensive, but when wisely administered, the doctrine strengthens the independence and self-government of private associations. Courts and administrative agencies should not interfere in the internal affairs of labor organizations, if union democracy is our goal, until the organization has had a reasonable opportunity to correct any mistakes of subordinate bodies.

It is not clear whether Section 101 (a) (4) affects both limitations upon suits by union members, or only the first, leaving the courts free to apply the exhaustion-of-remedies doctrine wherever appropriate. The sponsors of the bill of rights and other amendments adopted on the floor of the Senate were much less concerned with encouraging democratic self-government than were the supporters of the original Kennedy bills. The proviso permitting a union to require a man to exhaust internal remedies available within four months is more appropriately linked with the judicial doctrine than with restrictions imposed by a union. There are, however, a number of persuasive reasons for concluding that Section 101 (a) (4) was not intended to interfere with the exhaustion-of-remedies rule.

1. The words of Section 101 (a) (4) literally refer only to limitations imposed by a labor union, not to judicial rules of decision: "No *labor organization* shall limit the right of any member thereof to institute an

---

[72] *E.g.*, Constitution of the International Union, United Mine Workers of America, Art. IX.

[73] See Jackson,, J., dissenting in Trailmobile Co. v. Whirls, 331 U.S. 40, 69 (1947).

[74] 7 C.J.S. *Associations* §34(b).

[75] The labor cases are collected in Cox, *Rights Under a Labor Agreement*, 69 HARV. L. REV. 601, 647–49 (1956).

action in any court...."[76] It is obvious that Congress was concerned with union rules and union discipline interfering with the rights to testify and petition the legislature; the guaranty of the right to sue parallels these safeguards.

2. The exhaustion-of-remedies doctrine applies in the state courts no less than in federal forums. It seems unlikely that Congress would so lightly sweep aside state rules of judicial administration.

3. The broad interpretation would give Section 101 (a) (4) a curious backlash. If it regulates the legal proceedings brought by individual members by abolishing the exhaustion-of-remedies doctrine whenever the delay would exceed four months, must it not also regulate such proceedings by allowing unions to require any exhaustion of remedies which consume less than four months? If so, a labor union may now require a member to resort to proceedings within the union before filing charges under the NLRA; there was no such doctrine in the past.

4. Reading Section 101 (a) (4) to interfere with judicial and administrative rules of decision creates still other perplexities. It applies to all suits by union members regardless of the identity of the defendant. Does it therefore overturn the rule that an employee may not sue to enforce a collective bargaining agreement until he has exhausted the grievance procedure? Some labor contracts stipulate that no individual employee shall be entitled to any right or remedy outside the grievance procedure. In other cases unions negotiate adjustments intended to bind the grievants. To extend Section 101 (a) (4) into these areas would greatly interfere with collective bargaining.[77] Under the narrower interpretation the damage would not be done but the provision would still serve a useful and necessary purpose as a guarantee against restrictions imposed by union rules. Senator Kennedy's exposition of the Conference Report before the Senate vote espoused the latter meaning.

Viewed as a whole, the LMRDA relies primarily upon individual employees to enforce the duties of union officials. Many conscientious labor leaders and their legal advisers fear that the Act will result in a rash of burdensome litigation, some financed by employers despite the statutory prohibition,[78] which will waste the unions' resources and hamper their normal activities. On the other hand, there is the danger, often expressed in the past, that suits by individual employees are neither an effective sanction nor a practical remedy. Workers are unfamiliar with the law and hesitate to become involved in legal proceedings. The cost is likely to be heavy, and they have little money with

[76] Emphasis supplied.

[77] Cox, *supra* note 75.

[78] LMRDA §101(a)(4).

which to post bonds, pay lawyers' fees, and print voluminous records. Time is always on the side of the defendant. Even if the suit is successful, there are relatively few situations in which the plaintiff or his attorney can reap financial advantage. Most men are reluctant to incur financial cost in order to vindicate intangible rights. Individual workers who sue union officers run enormous risks, for there are many ways, legal as well as illegal, by which entrenched officials can "take care of" recalcitrant members.

Only time can resolve the uncertainty. Although the LMRDA creates few rights of action which did not exist at common law, their codification in highly publicized legislation will bring them to the attention of union members and their lawyers and, for a time at least, will both facilitate the litigation and reduce the fear of reprisals. Judges can be expected to respond to public and congressional opinion. Nevertheless, experience suggests that in the long run the volume of litigation will be quite small. Only two reported decisions involve suits for an accounting for alleged breach of an agent's fiduciary obligations.[79] Despite all the publicity, the large sums at stake, and the evidence developed by the McClellan Committee, there have been few actions against the Becks, Hoffas, Brewsters, and Webers of the labor movement. A hundredfold increase in the volume of litigation would not harm the labor movement. One of the proper costs of coming of age is the risk of unjustified litigation; the risk of unwarranted suits is the price we pay for assurance that every man will have his day in court.

III

Membership in a labor union reduces some aspects of individual liberty even when the union's activities are confined to collective bargaining, for under collective bargaining the individual employee must contribute whatever unique bargaining power he may have to the welfare of the group. By and large, however, the increased freedom which results from the power of an organized group generates opportunities for many other employees—freedom from the tyranny of poverty or the despotism of an arbitrary foreman, for example—which more than compensate for the occasional loss.

When a union embarks upon a program of political action, the threat to individual liberty is considerably greater. A worker who is free to participate in, and support, collective bargaining through the union of his choice while withholding support from political causes

[79] See note 25 *supra*.

advocated by the union, enjoys more freedom than one who is forced to choose between participating in collective bargaining and also supporting the union's political activities, on the one hand, and total abstention on the other.

But there are opposing considerations. It is difficult, if not impossible, to separate the economic and political functions of labor unions. Right-to-work laws affect union organization and collective bargaining. Legislation subjecting unions to the antitrust laws or confining their scope to the employees of a single company would greatly weaken their bargaining power, if it did not destroy them altogether. Although it seems unlikely that the LMRDA will seriously impair the strength of labor organizations, many union leaders hold an opposite view which time may prove correct. Political action in these spheres of union interest is hardly more than incidental to the unions' economic activities. A similar link exists even when a union takes political action upon a broader front. The basic philosophy of a President and his party affects appointments to agencies like the National Labor Relations Board, which in turn exert tremendous influence upon the course of labor relations. Even the tariff impinges on labor negotiations. The bargaining power of the Hatters Union, for example, is affected by the competition of low-cost foreign goods.

The participation of labor organizations in politics also carries affirmative values for the whole community. The influence of the unions is a counterpoise to the pressures generated by business interests. At their best unions bring to politics a strain of idealism reaching far beyond their own parochial interests, thus furnishing channels of expression for a constructive element of our national life. In practice, individual workers can do little to influence political decisions. Their opportunities are increased by the political activities of labor unions.

In theory, we could have the best of both worlds by forbidding collective bargaining representatives to engage in political activities and then permitting the organization of parallel political groups like PAC and COPE. In practice, the separation would be so unreal as to heap contempt upon the law. When a UAW vice-president delivers in Georgia during an election year an eloquent speech upon the need for stronger labor unions, he will inevitably be engaged both in spreading union organization and in calling for political action against sponsors of restrictive labor laws. Enforced separation would also weaken both the economic activities and the political influence of the labor movement. There are too few leaders, and too little money, for parallel organizations.

The federal law already provides for partial separation. The Taft-Hartley Act prohibits both corporations and labor organizations from making "a contribution or expenditure in connection with any Presidential or Congressional election."[80] Although the Supreme Court has construed the words strictly, with the result that unions continue to carry on many forms of political activity,[81] on balance it would seem unwise to enact broader legislation, or for a court to set aside the expulsion of a member who refused to pay nondiscriminatory assessments, approved by the majority, for political purposes. As the Supreme Court of California said in upholding the expulsion of Cecil B. De Mille from the American Federation of Radio Artists for refusing to pay a special assessment to finance a union campaign against a proposed right-to-work law:

> Dues and assessments paid by members to an association become the property of the association and any severable or individual interest therein ceases upon such payment.... Mere disagreement with the majority does not absolve the dissenting minority from compliance with action of the association taken through authorized union methods. The compliance—here payment by the plaintiff of the assessment—would not stamp his action as a personal endorsement of the declared view of the majority.[82]

The issue is closer when the worker is employed under a union-shop agreement. To force even an indirect political contribution as the price of retaining a job curtails one's freedom more severely than making the contribution a condition of union membership with the resulting opportunities for participation in collective bargaining; for fear of unemployment exerts stronger pressure than the desire to influence collective bargaining decisions. The question is now pending before the Supreme Court of the United States in constitutional form, in a case in which the Supreme Court of Georgia held unconstitutional the provision of the Railway Labor Act which authorizes carriers and the representatives of their employees to execute union-shop agreements notwithstanding any contrary state law.[83] The Georgia decision, which enjoined the enforcement of a union-shop agreement against the plaintiffs, was based upon an explicit finding that some of the dues which the plaintiffs would be required to pay as a condition of continued employment would be spent in support of political causes which the plaintiffs opposed.

---

[80] LMRA §304 amending §313 of the Corrupt Practices Act.

[81] United States v. C.I.O., 335 U.S. 106 (1948); *cf.* United States v. United Automobile Workers, 352 U.S. 567 (1957).

[82] De Mille v. American Fed'n of Radio Artists, 31 Cal. 2d 139, 149–50, 187 P.2d 769, 776 (1947).

[83] International Ass'n of Machinists v. Street, 108 S.E.2d 796 (Ga. 1959).

Enforcement of the contract would involve no violation of the First Amendment. The forced payment of dues does not curtail freedom of speech or association. It impairs no political rights. Since the only compulsion is to pay the regular dues—not an earmarked political assessment—the member does not even suffer the affront of being forced to pay money for an identifiable cause which he is unwilling to support. The reasoning of the *De Mille* case is pertinent upon this issue. The only serious constitutional argument, therefore, would seem to be that the statute plus the union-shop agreement takes the member's property without due process of law.

The Supreme Court has already decided that such compulsion to finance a union's economic activities is not arbitrary or capricious.[84] The impossibility of making a realistic allocation of a union's economic and political expenditures, coupled with the fact that only a small fraction of each dollar paid in general dues would normally go to finance political activities, would seem to furnish a rational foundation for the legislative judgment that no allocation should be required. These same considerations also persuade me that the statute is not unwise.

The law should prohibit efforts to coerce a union member in respect to his personal political activities. Since both the Taft-Hartley and Railway Labor Acts forbid the discharge of an employee under a union-shop agreement where his membership has been terminated for reasons other than the nonpayment of his regular dues,[85] there is no present likelihood that control over jobs can be used to influence workers' political activities. A case now pending in the California courts presents the closer question whether a union may lawfully expel men for political activities distasteful to the official hierarchy or to a majority of the members. Two members of the International Association of Machinists supported a proposed amendment to the California constitution in the 1958 election which would have outlawed closed- and union-shop agreements. Later they were charged with conduct unbecoming a union member. The trial board recommended expulsion. The verdict was upheld by the members of the local lodge. On appeal President A. J. Hayes sustained the expulsion, saying: "While it is agreed that the right to freely express one's views is a privilege guaranteed by the United States Constitution, this does not mean that a member of our association is entitled to openly denounce the considered position of the labor movement and particularly his own local, without the possibility of

[84] Railway Employees Department v. Hanson, 351 U.S. 225 (1956).

[85] NLRA §8(a)(3); RLA §2 Eleventh.

losing his rights to retain his standing as an I A of M Union member." The expelled members then brought an action for reinstatement. The trial court dismissed the complaint. An appeal is pending.[86]

The ultimate decision should turn upon analysis and appraisal of three elements in a complex situation. The first is, immediately, the importance of the individual's interest in union membership and, ultimately, its importance to the community. The union which acts as collective bargaining representative has the statutory power to fix the terms and conditions of employment of every employee in the bargaining unit. It controls the grievance procedure. The worker who is barred from union membership becomes bound by a contract negotiated without his participation or consent. For him talk about industrial democracy is sloganeering. If participation in industrial decisions is truly important to individual workers—and this is the basis of many pleas for support of collective bargaining—then threatening expulsion as the price of political nonconformity puts heavy pressure upon an employee to submerge his personal political views. And the community is also injured, if industrial democracy is a significant ideal.

The second important element in the complex is the interest of labor unions in confining their members to workers who are agreed upon the fundamental questions affecting them. No organization can be expected to harbor traitors. The Young Republican Clubs should not be prohibited from expelling members who have openly and repeatedly supported Democratic candidates for governor. Such a minority takes unfair advantage of its position, and the resulting dissension impairs the effectiveness of the organization. For many years labor unions were extraordinarily fragile. Dissent created strains which might easily cause disintegration. The risks of dissension were increased by the unions' vulnerability to attacks by employers. Conformity to group decisions was the price of survival. It seems doubtful, however, whether this factor should be given as much weight under modern conditions. Labor unions have achieved strength and stability. The centrifugal forces are counterbalanced by full-time officials, professional staffs, and, often, closely-knit internal organization. Furthermore, disagreement upon political issues, even upon the desirability of a right-to-work law, does not go to the heart of a labor union's functions. The member who acts as a strikebreaker may be guilty of treason, but one can believe in right-to-work laws and remain a good trade-unionist. There is even less need

[86] The Supreme Court of Tasmania reached the same conclusion under local legislation. Sykes, *An Industrial Law Goldmine: The Hursey Case*, 1 TASMANIAN L. REV, 175 (1959).

for conformity to the decisions of the majority upon other political issues, even though they affect the union's ability to perform its economic functions.

It needs no argument to demonstrate the importance of freedom to pursue personal political activities. It begs the question to say that a man has a right to engage in whatever political activity he wishes but no right to be a union member. The question is whether there will be an excessive loss of freedom if unions are permitted to make political conformity the price of membership. Bearing in mind the size and importance of unions in industry as well as their growing interest in politics, it seems apparent that the total loss would be great indeed if a significant number of large labor organizations adopted the attitude of the International Association of Machinists. It would also work serious changes in our political system if individuals can be insulated from direct political action by the decisions of organized groups even though the decisions are reached by majority rule.

On balance, the needs of the labor organizations seem insufficient to justify the curtailment of liberty which would result from allowing labor unions to expel members because of their political activity.

IV

The law can do much to enable union members to enforce the faithful performance of the fiduciary duties of elected officers. It can secure for workers the opportunity to take an active part in democratic unions without undue loss of political freedom. Although delicate judgments are involved, the law can also do something to protect the personal liberty of workers against improper pressure from the organization. Yet the most important qualities cannot be instilled by legislation or judicial decision. The law cannot compel members to assert their rights. It cannot teach them to view their unions as something more than service organizations hired to obtain benefits in return for dues. It cannot create the spirit of self-government or restore a sense of mission. The future of the labor movement probably depends less upon the course of legal developments than upon its capacity to feel and express the highest ideals of the community.

www.ingramcontent.com/pod-product-compliance
Lightning Source LLC
LaVergne TN
LVHW101441200926
848483LV00001B/8
9780313237942